A GUIDE TO
London's
BEST
Shops

DuCann

Published in association with
London Transport ⊖

First published in Great Britain in 1982 by Virgin Books Ltd., 95-99 Ladbroke Grove, London W11 1PG.

ISBN 0/907080/36/7

Printed in Great Britain by Richard Clay Ltd., Suffolk
Typesetting by Portobello Typesetting Ltd.
Designed by Dave Fudger
Illustrated by Patrick Cloonan
Production services by Book Production Consultants, Cambridge
Cover design by Ray Hyden
Distributed by Hamlyn Paperbacks.

CHARLOTTE DuCANN — THE AUTHOR

Charlotte DuCann was born in London in 1956; and read English at Birmingham University. She was a prize winner in Vogue's talent contest, subsequently working as their Shopping Editor for two years. She is now a freelance journalist for The Guardian, The Observer, The Mail on Sunday and the Sunday Express Magazine. Her interests include fashion, opera, claret and the 18th Century.

PATRICK CLOONAN — THE ILLUSTRATOR

Patrick Cloonan is a freelance illustrator.

ACKNOWLEDGEMENTS

I would like to thank Phil Webb, Andy Harris, Christian DuCann, Joanna Smith, Carey Smith and my long-suffering family for their help.

Virgin Books and the author would like to thank London Transport for their help in compiling this guide. Without their tireless efforts the invaluable transport sections of the guide could never have been completed.

PUBLISHER'S NOTE

The compiling of a guide under the title 'A Guide to London's Best' is bound to be a subjective and at times seemingly arbitrary exercise. We hope, however, that after countless hours of footwork and telephone checking, we have provided a reasonable selection of those shops in London that are worth travelling some distance to visit. Some of the better known names in the retail trade may seem conspicuous by their absence. However, this does not necessarily mean that they are not worth visiting but simply reflects the fact that they are everywhere and everybody knows where they are.

For the purposes of this guide London has been divided into sixteen areas, another exercise fraught with difficulties, and the areas have been ordered according to their geographical position, i.e. We start with **The West End** and then travel west to **Marylebone** and **Bayswater** and **Notting Hill**, turn south to **Fulham** and then go east to **Chelsea** and on to **East of the City** before turning north and west to **Islington**, **Camden** and **Hampstead**; finally south of the river is covered in two parts — **east** and **west**. Within each area the shops have been divided into product sections and listed alphabetically. For each shop the following information has been given: name, address, telephone number, and opening times. Each area is self-contained and completed with an introduction and illustration, a map and transport information and a few suggestions on where to rest one's tired feet.

Following the area section there is a product section dealing with specialist shops in a number of different fields and finally the indices, a product index and a shop index. Thus the guide will tell you where a shop is if you only know its name, where to go if you know what you want but not where to get it, and what there is in your particular locality.

Needless to say there will be errors, both of omission and of commission. If you know of a shop or service that we have failed to include but is worthy of mention, or disagree with those that have been included, or what has been written about them, please write and let us know. There is a form on the next page.

READERS RESPONSE FORM

To : Charlotte DuCann,
    'A Guide to London's BEST SHOPS'
    Virgin Books
    95/99 Ladbroke Grove
    LONDON W11 1PG

Name: ....

Address: ....

Telephone: ....

Comment: ....

....

....

....

....

....

....

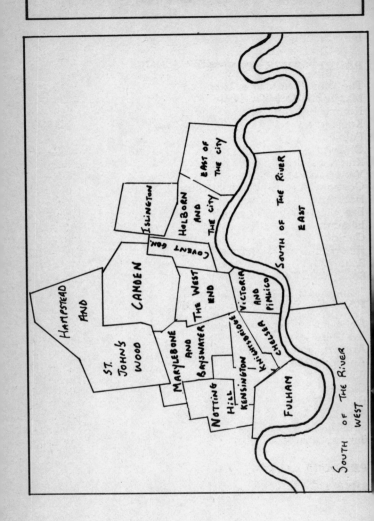

CONTENTS

Introduction

PART I — AREA SECTION

PART II — PRODUCT SECTION

PRODUCT INDEX
SHOP INDEX

AUTHOR'S INTRODUCTION

But why a shopping guide? Firstly for selfish reasons. After three years of writing about London shops, I thought if one more person flung me a question beginning with 'Where can I get...', I should go mad. Instead I wrote this book. Secondly I thought London needed a guide that wasn't either too worthy or entirely directed at credit card holders. It is written for those who think there is more to shopping than wheeling a supermarket trolley. Shopping for fun, style, fashion, good food, the finest quality (not necessarily the sharpest price), the wittiest ideas, the most helpful service, simply the best in a specialist field. The choice is unashamedly subjective. London is rich in shops but sometimes they are hard to winkle out. I hope this book will fling back the answers.

Charlotte DuCann

A GUIDE TO London's BEST Shops

PART I

AREA SECTION

WEST END

LINA STORES

The West End is a strange beast depending how you swing the shopping basket.

It can growl with bus, scream with people, be large, rude and cold, or it can appear as a quiet small thing, charming, well-polished, a fat cat. Its size defies definition — areas are neatly sliced like a vast Cheddar. Tottenham Court Road takes the utility furniture and video, the seedy streets of Soho some of the city's oldest and best delicatessens, fashion walks high in Bond Street, South Molton Street and St Christopher's Place, high street-wise in Oxford Street, tailored and specialist in Piccadilly. And like bulky lighthouses in a sea of plate glass, stand the great stores, Heals, Simpsons, Liberty's, Dickens and Jones, Debenhams' Selfridges with the main chainstore branches at their feet.

OXFORD STREET

O dear yes...Oxford Street, High Street of the metropolis, set between the unwanted monsters of two ages, Marble Arch and Centrepoint. There are some fine buildings in Oxford Street (do not miss the Barbara Hepworth sculpture incongruously set upon the side of John Lewis) but you would hardly notice them for the crowd that surges like a nightmare orchestrated by Fritz Lang. Oxford Street it is true has been massacred by the chain store, and peace offerings of green dustbins for the hamburger papers and spindly trees in concrete tubs do not atone for its ugliness. Every city in Britain has its cluster of chain stores although usually under a new roof, for which the demand cannot be denied. Find here a welter of Mothercare, Take Six, C&A, Littlewoods, British Home Stores, shoe shops such as Dolcis and Marks and Spencer and department stores like consumer battleships flanking the Northern side; Selfridges, Bournes, Debenhams and John Lewis.

CENTRES

Selfridges
Oxford St, W1 (629 1234)
Mon-Sat 9.30am-5.30, Thu
9.30am-7.00.
Selfridges steals the best facade and competes with Fortnum & Mason for the most glanced at clock in London.

The interior is notable for its food department and young sister Miss Selfridge. This most comprehensive branch has its own entrance in Duke St and is one of the best sources for high street fashion, especially for accessories, from berets to bags.

John Lewis
Oxford St, W1 (629 7711)
Mon-Sat 9.30am-5.30, Thu
9.30am-7.00.
John 'never knowingly undersold' Lewis abounds in practicality without losing its soul. The best place to find materials and a cheap kettle. Those in rigid blue are assistants.

West One
Oxford St, W1
A corner of soaring glass with marble concourse and shiny escalators with branches of **Top Shop, Top Man, Susan Reynolds, Holland & Barratt, Tomato,** *a sports shop and delicious chocolate kiosk. An alternative route to Bond St Station.*

Marks & Spencer
458 Oxford St, W1 (486 6151)
Mon-Fri 9.30am-5.30, Thu
9.30am-7.30, Sat 9.00am-5.00
This is the largest branch of M&S, commercial superstar, where the tills ring all day. Good honest knitwear and children's clothes, plus an extremely high quality, sometimes innovative supermarket. You won't be able to try any clothes on here but they do refund money if they don't fit.

Stephen Y
527-531 Oxford St, W1 (631 4771)
Mon-Tue 10.00am-6.00, Wed-Sat 9.30am-6.00, Thu 9.30am-7.30

Another hard-edged compilation Stephen Y has three storeys of middle fashion, children's clothes, stationery and cosmetics. Deposit shop-weary kids in the Play Area\and grab an unruffled cup of coffee in the upstairs cafe.

CLOTHES

Top Shop At Peter Robinson
Oxford Circus, W1 (636 7700)
Mon-Sat 9.30am-6.00, Thu 10.00am-8.00

Depending upon your concentration and strength, Top Shop can either appear as rails of bright, reasonable clothes or a psychedelic nightmare. Music thuds whilst the in-house disc jockey reels away the buys of the day. Top Shop sell their own label plus new innovations by Mechanic, Strawberry Studio, Miz etc.

FOOD

Paris Croissant
Oxford St, W1.
Mon-Sat 8.30am-7.30, Thu 8.30am-8.30

A tiny corner of civilisation next to HMV, fighting the hamburger with superb Gallic ease. Hot crisp croissants, broiches, croques dores, pains du chocolat...the street's best takeaway (you could always keep them for breakfast).

HOME

HMV
363 Oxford St, W1 (629 1240)
Mon-Fri 9.30am-6.30, Thu 9.30am-8.00; Sat 9.30am-6.00

HMV is vinyl paradise, despite the hellbent crowd. The largest record shop in Europe, HMV has three floors of records and one of tapes, musicals to musak. The classical music section is excellent. HMV will order anything you cannot find; keep a sharp eye for the changing discounts.

Virgin Megastore
14-16 Oxford St, W1 (636 1771)
Mon-Sat 10.00am-7.00

Rock supermarket with a quick ear for street beat. The place to go for imports and dynamic reductions on their weekly top fifty albums.

Games Centre
22 Oxford St, W1 (637 7911)
Mon-Sat 9.30am-10.00

Frantic shelves piled with board games from stalwarts like chess and Monopoly to the more esoteric war games, plus Rubiks smug little cubes, electronic mind-twisters and at this particular branch role-playing SF games, casino equipment and card tables. Also at 439 Oxford St, W1.

Lost Property Sales
113 Oxford St, W1 (434 4272)
Mon-Sat 9.30am-6.30, Thu 9.30am-8.00

All the relics of the Lost Property not claimed from 200 Baker St (London Transport) or British Rail (Waterloo Station) begins a new life here.

Umbrellas, suitcases, briefcases et al sit lonely and forlorn, amongst new discount trunks.

REGENT STREET

Regent Street has a less frenetic pace than Oxford Street, beginning gracefully at Dickens and Jones and ending with the tarnished blinking lights of Piccadilly. Here the shops are more stolidly well-heeled (Jaeger, Scotch House) and the Christmas lights once drew gasps of amazement. Living in a post-video age it is best to avoid disappointment and catch them from the top of the bus.

CENTRES

Liberty's
Regent St, W1 (734 1234)
Mon- Fri 9.00am-5.30, Thu
9.00am-7.00, Sat 9.00am-5.00
Liberty has the nostalgic charm that most department stores lack, partly due to its quirky half-timbered facade in Great Marlborough St and inner oak panelling but mostly to the feeling of rolls of rich cloth and spices unloaded when the winds of trade blew more fair. Upstairs for the famous Liberty prints, varuna wools and Tana lawns, downstairs for their modern furniture, Oriental Bazaar and One-Off department which holds exhibitions of fine crafts.

CHILDREN

Hamleys
188 Regent St, W1 (734 3161)
Mon-Sat 9.00am-5.30
Hamleys is the biggest toyshop in the world and has recently invaded larger premises designed by the Disneyland team (more utility than magic) The range of toys are as jumbled as a Christmas stocking. There is a sports department on the Third Floor and a rejuvenating cafe on the fourth. The omission of prim 'Do Not Touch' signs makes this a great place to bring children depending upon patience.

CLOTHES

Acquascutum
100 Regent St, W1 (734 6090)
Mon-Sat 9.00am-5.30, Thu
9.00am-7.00
For men of tradition (the rich sober sort not the fusty). The raincoats and tweed jackets are still famous. See also **Austin Reed** *across the road.*

Warehouse Utility Clothing Co
19/21 Argyll St, W1 (437 7101)
Mon-Sat 9.30am-6.30, Thu
9.30am-8.00
Sharp buying from manufacturers with cut labels and further cut prices, small range but furious turnover makes this a success. Best for silks, utility cotton and accessories (socks, leather belts, stripey umbrellas). There are branches throughout London,

13

this is the largest. Also at 202 Earls Court Rd, SW5; 143 Holborn, EC1; 99a Cheapside, EC2; 27 Duke St, W1.

Roots
4 Conduit St, W1 (493 4555)
Mon-Fri 10.00am-6.00, Sat 10.00am-5.30
Grab your ideological boots here. Backward sloping the original shoes are not beautiful but they're supposed to do brilliant things for the spine.

Jaeger
204-206 Regent St, W1 (734 8211)
Mon-Sat 9.30am-5.30, Thu 9.30am-7.00
For the eternal classic, suits, straighter skirts, shirts, flannel, tweed, pinstripe and navy blue.

FOOD

Danish Food Centre
12 Conduit St, W1 (499 7040)
Mon-Fri 9.00am-6.00, Sat 9.00am-5.00
Best bacon, yoghurt drinks, variegated crispbreads and pickled fish for northern palates. The open sandwiches are a cumbersome but civilised take-away.

HOME

Mitsukiku
90 Regent St, W1 (437 5582)
Mon-Sat 10.00am-6.00, Thu 10.00am-7.00
Mitsukiku swinging with coloured paper lampshades, sells all things Japanese, massage sticks and sandals, futons, screens, rice bowls for low tables, kites for high skies. The mainsong is the kimono bright and happy to intensely embroidered silk. Who said Madame Butterfly was dead? Also at 4 Pembridge Rd, W11; 15 Old Brompton Rd, SW7; 157 Victoria St, SW1; 435 Strand, WC2; 26 North Audley St, W1; 209 Kensington High St, W8.

Pencraft
119 Regent St, W1 (734 4928)
Mon-Sat 9.00am-5.30, Sat 9.00am-5.30
Vast cases of pens for ink-freaks to dip into. Engraving and repairs (for old and new pens).

BOND STREET

Bond Street is lined with a thick golden carpet and the discreet glitter of the assistant's smile. Designer names drop like pearls (Dior, Gucci, Yves St Laurent, Loewe, Ted Lapidus) mixed with the richest shoe leather (Rayne, Ferragamo, Midas) and jewellers of the rocky kind (find the flagship at Asprey). Glitterati find the Art in Cork Street and cut the bespoke cloth in Savile Row.

CENTRES

Fenwicks
63 New Bond St, W1 (629 9161)
Mon-Fri 9.00am-6.00; Thu 9.00am-7.30, Sat 9.00am-5.30.
Small clothes department store with a medium price stage. Cafe, hairdresser, cosmetics, stationery but best for accessories.

The White House
51/2 New Bond St, W1 (629
3521)
Mon-Fri 9.00am-5.30, Sat
9.00am-1.00.
*Specialists in linen of the fine
and expensive kind. The
White House has an incredibly
calm and anachronistic
interior. Very good for lawn
handkerchiefs and those
Harris tweed coats with velvet
collars for well-behaved
children.*

BOOKS

Chappell
50 New Bond St, W1 (491
2777)
Mon-Fri 9.30am-6.00, Sat
9.30am-5.00.
*London's largest supplier of
sheet music, classical to rock,
teaching methods and opera
scores. Chappell also sell
pianos and organs.*

CLOTHES

Crolla
35 Dover St, W1 (629 5931)
Mon-Sat 10.00am-6.00, Thu
10.00am-7.00.
*One of the best men's clothes
shops in the city. Modern
English classics in unexpected
colours. Striped shirts, argyle
socks, amazing ties and bow
ties, silk cummerbunds,
dinner suits, brocade slippers,
shiny leather shoes.*

Elle
92 New Bond St, W1 (629
4441)
Mon-Fri 10.00am-6.30, Thu
10.00am-7.30, Sat 10.00am-5.30.
*Excellent Italian and French
designed clothes, Ventilo,
Kamikaze etc. The price tag is
always depressing.*

Fiorucci
133 New Bond St, W1 (491
3499)
Mon-Fri 10.00am-6.30, Thu
10.00am-7.30, Sat 10.00am-6.00.
*Bold, bright, fun, witty,
Fiorucci splash colour on
clothes, stationery, gumboots,
sunglasses. Always innovative,
often over-priced.*

Ireland House Shop
150 New Bond St, W1 (493
6219)
Mon-Fri 9.15am-5.30, Thu
9.15am-6.00, Sat 9.15am-4.00.
*Takes the best cloth from the
Emerald Isle, Donegal tweed,
thick Aran sweaters, vivid
plaid rugs/shawls. Some
designed by Dublin whizz-kid
Paul Costelloe. Waterford
glass downstairs.*

Herbert Johnson
13 Old Burlington St, W1 (439
7397/8/9) Mon-Fri 9.00am-5.00,
Sat 9.00am-4.00.
*The proper hats for huntin',
shootin' and fishin'; bowlers
for gentlemen of the city,
fedoras for the flamboyant.
Do not miss the regimental
striped stable belts and
spotted silk handkerchiefs.
Women's hats downstairs.*

Ralph Lauren
143 New Bond St, W1 (629
3249)
Mon-Sat 10.00am-6.00, Thu
10.00am-7.00.
*Old chemist redesigned by
Robin and Tricia Guild where
the preppie meets the prairie.*

15

Navajo knits and soft tweeds for women, the Polo range for men.

Anthony Lloyd Jennings
7 Old Bond St, W1 (491 7974)
Mon-Fri 9.00am-6.00.
Anthony Lloyd Jennings make all their shoes on their own lasts, brogues to black patent riding boots to order. Very English, excellent service.

Janet Reger
12 New Bond St, W1 (493 8357)
Mon-Fri 10.00am-6.00, Sat 10.00am-5.00.
Where lingerie lingers, frilled, white lace, satin and silks plus floating chiffon nightdresses. Not for the realist. Also at 2 Beauchamp Place, SW3.

Zandra Rhodes
14a Grafton St, W1 (499 3596/6695)
Mon-Fri 9.30am-6.00, Sat 9.30am-5.00.
The lady of the shocking pink hair and innovative fabrics sells the ballgown for the outrageous night.

HOME

The Cocktail Shop
5 Avery Row, W1 (493 9744)
Mon-Sat 10.00am-6.00.
For those who take their Negronis seriously. The Cocktail Shop offers all the shiny correct machinery: shakers, strainers, stirrers and ice buckets for the perfect glass. The less than purist decorate theirs with swizzle sticks and pink umbrellas, buy the witty guide and stationery and cheat with the exotic powder mixes.

Culpeper
21 Bruton St, W1 (499 2406)Mon-Fri 9.30am-6.00 (Thu 7.00), Sat 10.00am-6.00.
First of the city's herbalists before everybody went natural and wholemeal. Culpeper sell the herbs medicinal, culinary and cosmetic, pot pourri from many gardens and scented pillows.

Smythson
54 New Bond St, W1 (629 8558)
Mon-Fri 9.30am-5.30, Sat 9.15am-12.30.
The Regal stationers, Smythson's sell the best headed notepaper, visiting cards, sealing wax and leather-bound diaries. Where to go to get your Game Book.

FOOD

Charbonnel & Walker
1 Royal Arcade, 28 New Bond St, W1 (629 4396/5149)
Mon-Fri 9.00am-5.30, Sat 10.00am-1.00.
Mlle Charbonnel, Parisian chocolatiere was brought to London by the Prince of Wales to delight the jaded palates of those who could afford her creme de la creme. Famous for boites blanches with messages written in gold-wrapped chocolates.

SPORTS

Giddens
15d Clifford St, W1 (734 2788)

Mon-Fri 9.00am-5.00, Sat 10.00am-1.00.
Where the urban gentry collect their tack. Upstairs for jewel-bright polo shirts, riding bowlers, breeches and ankle boots. Riding boots made to measure.

ST. CHRISTOPHER'S PLACE

No one likes to be bullied into a habit, least of all shoppers who swing a conservative basket. St Christopher's Place launched with a party of fireworks as another fashion paved zone, still fights hard for acceptance. Suffering from appearing to be South Molton Street's country cousin and lacking its fine cafe bustle The Place nevertheless springs some great shops and tiny restaurants (see the Nouveau Cafe Crowd take the cocktail in the pink surrounds at the Coconut Grove) and Barratt Street Antique Market houses many a collector surprise.

CHILDREN

Anastasia
28 James St, W1 (935 0446)
Mon-Fri 10.00am-7.00, Thu 10.00am-8.00, Sat 10.00am-5.30.
Traditional English children's clothes inspired by old times when the playground was the nursery and there was always toast for tea. Classic party dresses in tartan, velvet with antique lace, knickerbockers in Harris tweed and sailor suits.

CLOTHES

Artwork
33 St Christopher's Place, W1 (486 4733)
Mon-Sat 10.00am-6.00, Thu 10.00am-7.00.
As the name implies, the knitwear here is more than just an odd sweater. Beaded, glittered, graffitied, never boring, frequently expensive.

Margaret Howell
25/6 St Christopher's Place, W1 (935 8588)
Mon-Sat 10.00am-6.00, Thu 10.00am-7.00, Sat 10.00am-5.00.
Force of the modern English classic, Margaret Howell is the best place to gather the Fair Isles, wing collars, jewel-piped pyjamas, fishing corduroy, braces, fine shirting and suiting. No 25 for men, no 26 for women.

Mulberry Co
32 St Christopher's Place, W1 (486 3052)
Mon-Sat 10.00am-6.00, Thu 10.00am-7.00.
Mulberry is famous for its bags, mostly leather, taken away from the prim image. Accessorise madly here with belts, brollies, beach wear and bow ties.

Paddy Campbell
8 Gees Court, St Christopher's Place, W1 (493 5646)
Mon-Sat 10.00am-6.00, Thu 10.00am-7.00.
Individual designer for the demure well-cut skirt and dress, navy wool, Liberty print and Viyella. Upstairs for evening.

Teamwork
12 St Christopher's Place, W1
(487 4484)
Mon-Sat 10.00am-6.30, Thu
10.00am-7.00.
*Teamwork perhaps typifies the
St Christophers Place style
with up-front fashion for those
who change according to
season rather than sense. Take
away the best of Mitchicko,
Miz, Swanky Modes and Paul
Howie.*

HOME

Cutler & Gross
18 St Christophers Place, W1
(486 4079)
Mon-Sat 10.00am-6.00, Thu
10.00am-7.00.
*Every kind of specs from
Harvard tortoishell to the
wildest pink and rhinestone
batwings. Cutler & Gross
travel the world for designs
and colour the frame in any
colour. One glance and your
lost. Expensive but then so are
all English glasses, unless you
go National Health.*

SOUTH MOLTON STREET

*South Molton Street is the
city's catwalk set between the
maelstrom of Oxford Street
and the coutured calm of
Bond Street. At one end the
bright beautiful people
appear, throw their
reflections in shop windows,
catch a glance from the cafe
voyeurs, then disappear
mysteriously at the other. It is
a place to be seen in,
frequented by the right
people where fashion stalks*
*like a precocious child with
no traffic to get in the way.*

ANTIQUES

Grays Antique Market
Grays In The Mews, 1-7
Davies St, W1 (493 7861) Grays
In The Street 58 Davies St, W1
(629 7034)
Mon-Fri 10.00am-6.00.
*Vast space crammed with
antiques of the more
decorative sort, especially
Victoriana, Oriental rugs, Art
Nouveau and Deco, books and
ephemera. Look out for the
stall of cats, Ritva Westerius
for lace and Tessa Hughes for
textiles. Both markets have
cafes of the quicher kind.*

CHILDREN

Zero 4
53 South Molton St, W1 (493
4920)
Mon-Fri 10.00am-6.00, Sat
10.00am-5.00.
*Very French and Italian
clothes for children more
sportif than spoilt. Sell their
own jumpers and accessories.
From babies to awkward
teenagers.*

CLOTHES

Benetton
6 South Molton St, W1 (629
0546)
Mon-Sat 10.00am- 6.00,
Thu 10.00am-7.00.
*Modern classic knits with a
clever Italian cut. Find the
plain bright colours in a
myraid of jumpers, ribbed*

*tight scarves, pullover and jump dress plus Viyella check shirts, tartan mix kilts and simple cotton corduroy. All the knitwear is stacked on shelves which looks amazing but can be a problem if you're in an indecisive mood. (See also their children's shop **012** at 22 South Molton St)*

Browns
23, 25-27 South Molton St, W1 (491 8733)
Mon-Fri 10.00am-6.00,
Thu 10.00am-7.00,
Sat 10.00am-5.00.
The designers' place. A fanfare facade of cool cocoa and cream — no 23 for men, no 27 for women, no 25 for shoes, no 24 and 26 for dash hits the American Calvin Klein and the Italian Giorgio Armani (and with its own entrance in Davies St, The Missoni Shop for the multisprinkled knit) Browns takes the cloth straight from the collections, cutting bias towards the dynamic American designers rather than the classic Parisian couture. If you want it now be prepared to pay the price. Stable includes Thierry Mugler, Perry Ellis, Montana, Halston, Maud Frizon, Pinky & Diane, OMO, Norma Kamali and Brown's own label.

Ebony
45 South Molton St, W1 (408 1247)
Mon-Sat 10.30am-6.00, Thu 10.30am-7.00.
Men's clothes with rich bite and colour. Accessories and hand knits. For show offs who need to.

Joseph
13 South Molton St, W1 (493 4420)
Mon-Sat 10.00am-6.00, Thu 10.00-7.00.
One of the sharpest and most amusing fashion shops in London — strong visuals and quick turnover (keep an eye for Katherine Hamnett utility wear). See also no 14 for shoes.

Santini e Domenici
14 South Molton St, W1 (629 9617)
Mon-Sat 9.30am-6.00, Thu 9.30am-7.00.
— recognize them for the stripey shoe boxes and dashing boots, and no 16 for the designer collection, especially Kenzo.

Monsoon
67 South Molton St, W1 (499 3987)
Mon-Sat 10.00am-6.00, Thu 10.00am-8.00.
If you take it, Oriental hand blocked cotton and silk of the best sort. Dresses to float and glitter in the romantic (sic) night.

Rider
8 South Molton St, (493 8953)
Mon-Sat 10.00am-6.00, Thu 10.00am-7.00.
Innovative shoe shop with streamlined shelves. From the straightest court to costume footage. Labels include Acceccesoire, Soda, Tokio, Walkers and the upper cut of Pancaldi. Prices equally diverse.

Trussardi
51 South Molton St, W1 (629 5611)

Mon-Sat 9.30am-6.00, Thu
9.30am-7.00.
*Trussardi has the kind of
luggage that only travels on Le
Train Bleu or the Orient
Express. Especially good for
huge soft leather bags in
primrose, navy or white and
their briarwood and silver
pens. Leather clothes and
boots downstairs. Great style,
shame about the price.*

FOOD

Prestat
24 South Molton St, W1 (629
4838)
Mon-Sat 9.00am-6.00, Sat
9.00am-5.00.
*Really decadent
chocolates...three kinds of
truffle, rose and violet creams,
silver almonds and orange
bombes to blow your
tastebuds. Prestat will also
send chocolate telegrams and
sculpt special commissions.*

HR Higgins
42 South Molton St, W1 (499
5912)
Mon-Wed 8.45am-5.30, Thu
8.45am-7.00, Fri 8.45am-6.00.
*The old coffee man of South
Molton Street, established in
excellence since 1943.*

PICCADILLY
& ST. JAMES'S

*Piccadilly Circus is one of
those city magnets, like
Broadway, where no amount
of bright lights and legend
can make up for the dark and
cruel pavements that are their
truth. Piccadilly, the street, is
another land, shining with the
Airways glass, the painterly
portals of the Royal Academy,
the sweet Fortnums clock, the
fine facade and quiet interior
of St James, Wren's other
church. Connected by
dazzling arcades, Jermyn
Street echoes another time
when civility bowed a
deferential head and some
took tea at the Ritz or at their
clubs that line the Mall and
read the papers in the
Reading Room of the London
Library, St James Square.*

BOOKS

Hatchards
187 Piccadilly, W1 (439 9921)
Mon-Fri 9.00am-5.30, Sat
9.00am-1.00.
*The oldest booksellers in
London, carpeted and well-
staffed. Selective paperbacks,
art books, antequarian and
hardback new fiction.*

Heywood Hill
10 Curzon St, W1 (629 0647)
Mon-Fri 9.00am-5.30, Sat
9.00am-12.30.
*Literary general bookshop
once run by Nancy Mitford
and specialising in Eng Lit
(sans academe) antiquarian
and children's books, all
beautifully and carefully
chosen. Heywood Hill know
most of their customers and all
of their books. The service is
excellent.*

CLOTHES

Burberry's
18 Haymarket, SW1
(930 3343)

Mon-Sat 9.00am-5.30, Thu
9.00am-7.00.
The Raincoat.

James Drew
3 Burlington Arcade, W1 (493
0714)
Mon-Fri 9.00am-5.30, Sat
9.00am-12.45.
*The immaculate but expensive
women's shirt, especially good
for silks,wing and pierrot collars.*

Lobbs
9 St James St, SW1 (930 3664)
Mon-Fri 9.00am-5.30, Sat
9.00am-1.00.
*One of the last true shoe-
makers in this land with each
customer's last cut in wood and
every piece of leather
fashioned by hand. The prices
are no fairy tale.*

Locks
6 St James St, SW1 (930 8874)
Mon-Fri 9.00am-5.00, Sat
9.30am-12.30.
*The gentleman's hat, tweedy
and deerstalker for a winter's
bracken, panama and boater
for a summer's haze, and of the
top hat. Where the first bowler
was made.*

N Peal
37 Burlington Arcade, W1 (493
5378)
Mon-Fri 9.00am-5.30, Sat
9.00am-1.00.
*Classic cashmere in every
shade of the woollen rainbow
— ruanas baggy breeks,
pullovers, hand-loomed
intarsia, mufflers. Give the
twinset a break.*

Turnbull & Asser
71/72 Jermyn St, SW1 (930
0502)

Mon-Fri 9.00am-5.30, Sat
9.00am-1.00.
*Great shirtmakers in English
cotton and silk. Striped silk
pyjamas, velvet smoking
jackets, spotted cravats; for the
made to measure shirts go
next door to no 23 Bury St.*

John Baily
116 Mount St, W1 (499 1833)
Mon-Fri 7.30am-4.00.
*One of the city's great tiled
facades, swinging with game
their speciality (hunt the rare
bird here). The country's
oldest poulterers. Free range.*

Fortnum & Mason
181 Piccadilly, W1 (734 8040)
Mon-Sat 9.00am-6.00.
*Although Fortnum's has other
rooms it is most famous for its
food department, a god's
hamper served with conscious
civility by tail-coated assistants.
'I only eat fruit out of season'
declared Pinero and Fortnums
provides accordingly.
Outrageous ice cream sundaes
in the Fountain Bar.*

Paxton & Whitfield
93 Jermyn St, SW1 (930 0259)
Mon-Fri 8.30am-5.00, Sat
8.30am-12 noon.
*Hymn to the great English
cheese (forget the
supermarket brie), rare
regionals, wheels of Stilton
and cheddar to bite your
tongue off. Wide range of
Continental cheese,
especially fragrant French
goat's and six different
cures   of ham on the
bone.*

21

HOME

Astleys
109 Jermyn St, SW1 (930 1687)
Mon-Fri 9.00am-6.00, Sat
10.00am-1.00.
*Victorian pipe palace. Briars,
antiques and repairs.*

Boots
Criterion Building, Piccadilly,
W1 (930 4761)
Mon-Sat 8.30am-8.00.
*The biggest and most central
chemist in the city.*

Design Centre
28 Haymarket, SW1 (839
8000)
Mon-Sat 9.30am-5.30, Thu
9.30am-9.00.
*By the sign of the black and
white label, buy the design that
is good for you. Retail shop of
Government approved
designed objects and
exhibitions. Since the choice
has already been made,
possibly the least exciting shop
in London.*

Floris
89 Jermyn St, SW1 (930 2885)
Mon-Fri 9.30am-5.30.
*Old fashioned toilet waters
and perfumes established
since the 18th C. Those who
take the bathroom seriously
buy the quintessential rose
mouthwash, ivory hairbrush,
tortoiseshell comb, natural
sponge, badger toothbrush,
pomander ball and lavender
water.*

Fribourg & Treyer
34 Haymarket SW1 (930 1305)
Mon-Sat 9.00am-5.00.
*If you pinch it, snuff in its
infinite itchy variety. Cigars
and olde worlde Georgian
bow fronted window.*

Irish Linen
35 Burlington Arcade, W1 (493
8949)
Mon-Fri 9.00am-5.30, Sat
9.00am-1.00.
*For a plainer serving of bed
and table. Pure white damask
for heavy evenings, organdie
for lighter luncheons. Swiss
lawn and French lace
handkerchiefs.*

Sullivan Powell
34 Burlington Arcade, W1 (629
0433)
Mon-Fri 9.00am-5.30, Sat
9.00am-1.00.
*Founded in the 19th C by
Jonathan Sullivan, Master
Mariner, eager to convert the
nobility to the exotic flavour of
the Oriental cigarette. Still
great for the Turkish oval
smoke but the sampling of
tobaccos and the ladies that
hand-rolled cigars above the
shop have gone the way of
nostalgia.*

SPORTS

Lillywhites
Piccadilly Circus, W1 (930
3181)
Mon-Sat 9.30am-6.00, Thu
9.30am-7.00.
*The All Sports department
store, for clothes and
equipment. Stylists play
croquet amongst the burnished
leaves, sport baggy cricket
whites and wave-glo plastic
sailing trousers, Speedo
swimming costumes and shiny
boxer or running shorts.*

Swaine, Adeney, Briggs & Sons

185 Piccadilly, W1 (734 4277)
Mon-Fri 9.00am-5.30, Sat
9.00am-4.30.
Best whips of the hunting sort, spurs, bits, hacking and tacking for the horsey crust.

Captain OM Watts

45 Albemarle St, W1 (493 4633)
Mon-Fri 9.00am-5.30, Sat
9.00am-1.00.
The city's chandlers — logs, compasses, outboards, inflatable dinghies, charts and books for braving the deep. At no 42 the clothing for sailpersons and vail landlubbers, wet suits, raw sweaters of Breton stripe and blue fisher captains hats, reefer jackets and bright yellow wellingtons.

SOHO

Soho is always a journey, rich and strange. Surrounded by the commercial highways of Oxford Street, Regent Street and the bookish theatrical Charing Cross Rd, Soho is a mesh of small streets whirling with broken cabbage leaf and old newspaper. Its inhabitors are all drunkards and jazzmakers, film producers, journalists, art students, refugees, poets, punters, photographers and pornographers. These last have probably saved Soho from being trendy, quaint or rebuilt but are still strangling its life. Soho has never been nice but the traveller could still hear the wild cries of the fruit markets, see the salami swinging delicatessen windows, smell the bizarre cauldrons of Chinatown and feel he had arrived.

BOOKS

The Vintage Magazine Store

Brewer St, W1 (439 8525)
Mon-Thu 10.30am-6.30, Fri-Sat
10.30am-8.00.
The ephemera emporium. Upstairs, recent magazines, rock, sport, newspapers, back numbers of Private Eye; downstairs, pre-1950 collection, Boys' Own, Hollywood stills in Film Section, old Vogues in Fashion, posters and framing service.

CHILDREN

Galt Toys

30 Great Marlborough St, W1
(734 0829)
Mon-Fri 9.00am-5.30, Sat
9.00am-5.00.
Set on the corner of the appalling Carnaby St, all T-shirts and reproduction pub mirrors. Here Galt keep their entire range of educational and chunky toys and games.

CLOTHES

P Denny

39 Old Compton St, W1 (437 1654)
Mon-Fri 8.45am-5.30.
Denny's have been supplying the restaurant trade with uniforms for years. If you take utility wear, grab the essential blue checked trousers, sky-blue overalls, white bib and braces and mess jackets.

23

Gamba
46 Dean St, W1 (437 0704)
Mon-Fri 9.00am-5.30, Sat
9.00am-1.00.
*Theatrical shoes. Toe-tappers
get their dance feet here —
ballet, tap, jazz and character
in a myriad of colours.*

The Fabric Studio
10 Frith St, W1 (494 2897)
Mon-Sat 10.00am-6.00.
*Rolls of bargain cloth from
pinstripe to kitsch florals,
suedes, lining silks, buttons,
remnants and trimmings.*

FOOD

Algerian Coffee Stores
52 Old Compton St, W1 (437
2480)
Tue-Sat 9.00am-5.30.
*Great red facade. Do not
believe the name — they sell
other coffees and teas, coffee
machines and coffee sacks.*

Berwick Street and Rupert Street Markets
Mon-Sat 9.00am-5.00.
*Fruit and veg, cheap and fresh.
Easy however to get carried
away in the brash streetiness of
it all and forget about quality.
Don't end up with four pounds
of soggy tomatoes no matter
how much of a bargain. Rupert
St Market has a few other stalls
for shoes, fabric and records.*

Cranks Health Foods
8 Marshall St, W1 (437 9431)
(24hr ansafone 734 4640)
Mon-Fri 9.00am-6.00, Sat
9.00am-4.30.
*Wholefood supermarket, next
to Cranks Restaurant. Goats'
milk products, carrot juice,
vitamins, free range eggs.
Meat eating decadents would
feel the loss.*

Cranks Whole Grain Shop
37 Marshall St, W1 (349 1809)
Mon 10.00am-6.00,
Sat 10.00am-4.00.
*Sacks of purist grains and
pulses for the bean brigade,
plus two sorts of the
redoubtable muesli. Don't
forget Marshall St Swimming
Baths opposite to complete the
programme.*

Dugdale & Adams
3 Gerrard St, W1 (437 3864)
Mon-Sat 8.00am-4.00.
*The best French loaf made in
London, baked underground
in Victorian ovens. Plus other
white crusties.*

Great Wall
31-37 Wardour St, W1 (437
7963)
Mon-Sat 11.00am-8.00.
*Chinese and Japanese food
store awash with woks and
beancurd.*

The House Of Floris
39 Brewer St, W1 (437 5755)
Mon-Fri 9.00am-5.30, Sat
9.00am-1.00.
*Specialists of the old and
grand celebration cake.
Ribboned boxes of hand-made
chocolates, pastries and
croissants.*

Lina Stores
18 Brewer St, W1 (437 4728)
Mon-Sat 8.00am-6.00, Thu
8.00am-1.00.
*Everything an Italian
delicatessen should be for
those who crave the sun.
Panetone festooned ceiling,*

crusty bread at the steamy window, excellent black olives, thick green oil, rough salamis, dried herbs and dark bitter coffees.

Loon Fung Supermarket
39/42-43 Gerrard St, W1 (437 1922)
11.00am-9.00 seven days a week.
Huge and extraordinary store selling all the Oriental diverse foodstuffs — water chestnut starch to dried fishes, fresh fruit and veg, Chinese sweets to kitchen equipment and crockery. Package freaks will love it.

G Parmigiani Figli
43 Frith St, W1 (437 4728)
Mon-Sat 9.00am-5.00, Thu 9.00am-1.00.
Streamlined Italian delicatessen with an enormous selection of Italian cheeses.

Randall & Aubin
16 Brewer St, W1 (437 3507)
Mon-Sat 8.30am-5.00, Thu 8.30am-12 noon.
Great butchers specialising in French cuts of meat with sausages, pies, salamis, pates and groceries. Old-fashioned and chaotic.

Richards
11 Brewer St, W1 (437 1358)
Tue-Sat 8.00am-5.15.
The fish man of Soho. Where to get monk fish and oysters and live crab.

Slater and Cooke, Bisney and Jones
67 Brewer St, W1 (437 2026)
Mon-Fri 8.00am-5.00.
High-tech butchers with little

metal chairs, tiles and separate counters for each kind of meat. Decoratively prepared meat, especially paupiettes de veau, haggis and game. The most graphic butchers in London.

HOME

Anything Left Handed
68 Beak St, W1 (437 3910)
Mon-Fri 10.00am-5.00, Sat 10.00am-5.00.
A rare shop, specialising in tools for the maligned left-hander. The stock includes tin openers, scissors, potato peelers and pens for calligraphy. The special mugs are confusing.

Craftsmen Potters Association
William Blake House, Marshall St, W1 (437 7605)
Mon-Fri 10.00am-5.30, Sat 10.00am-4.00.
Don't be deceived by the address, William Blake certainly did not live in such an unpoetic building. Functional and decorative pottery scrupulously selected. Much brownish stoneware, some slipware. Books and tools.

Harold Moore's Records
2 Marlborough St, W1 (437 1576)
Mon-Sat 10.00am-6.00, Sun 12 noon-7.00.
Excellent source of classical records, plus deletions, rare records, bargains and second hand.

William Page
87 Shaftesbury Ave, WC2 (960 2121)

Mon-Fri 9.30am-5.30.
Restaurant suppliers. If you look beyond the giant saucepans and rows of stainless steel jugs you can find tough multiple toasters, utility glass, terrifying knives and other kitchen efficiency. The best (and cheapest) place to buy a cocktail shaker.

Stuffed
23 Beak St, W1 (439 7311)
Mon-Sat 10.00am-6.00.
Pretty on visuals, whimsical on content, animals and objects in stuffed satin, cushions to spiders and giant toothpaste tubes. Frogs a speciality, commissions taken.

The Yarn Store
8 Ganton St, W1 (734 4532)
Tue-Fri 10.00am-6.00, Thu 10.00am-7.00, Sat 11.00am-6.00.
Modern wool place (as opposed to the granny sort) where a jumper becomes a hand-knit. Donegal, chenille and the main song Superchunky in rainbow colours. Patterns for each wool designed by one of the owners who teaches at the Royal College of Art.

TOTTENHAM COURT ROAD

Tottenham Court Road is Video Street — dials and machines along a stretch of cold wind-pitted concrete and glass. Every system can be found here, expensively or for a sharp price. Further towards Euston, the furniture takes over, ending with Maples, temple of the three piece suite and a small

civilized pocket called Fitzrovia full of restaurants, art galleries and delicatessens.

CHILDREN

Pollock's Toy Museum
1 Scala St, W1 (636 3452)
Mon-Sat 10.00am-5.00.
One of the most enchanting shops in London. Upstairs the Toy Museum, downstairs the cut-out theatres for which they are famous, Victorian scraps, toys of traditional wood and Chinese tin.

FOOD

Ferns
27 Rathbone Place, W1 (636 2237)
Mon-Sat 7.00am-5.00.
Wooden-lined old fashioned tea and coffee shop, equipment and coffee sugars. Also at The Market, Covent Garden, WC2 and 16 High St, Barnes, SW13.

Bartholdi
4 Charlotte St, W1 (636 3762)
Mon-Sat 9.00am-6.00, Sat 9.00am-1.00.
Swiss butchers with continental cuts, smoked meats, holey cheese and Alpine biscuits.

HOME

Adeptus
110 Tottenham Court Rd, W1 (388 5965)
Mon-Sat 10.00am-6.00, Thu 10.00am-7.30.

Seats, sofas and beds in that bleak functional foam rubber. The shop is pure Caulfield.

Byzantium
1 Goodge St, W1 (636 6465)
Mon-Fri 10.00am-6.00, Sat 10.00am-5.00.
Striped rugs, shepherd-thick jumpers, brass plate, cushions and raw leather sandals and crimson slippers from the Greek east.

Chivers
127 Tottenham Court Rd, W1 (387 6996)
24 hour refrigerated flowers. Also at 143 Charlotte St, W1 and 68 Marchmont St, WC1.

Habitat
156 Tottenham Court Rd, W1 (388 1721)
Mon 9.30am-7.00, Tue, Wed, Fri 9.30am-5.30, Sat 9.30am-6.00.
The acceptable face of modernism. It is difficult to think of a time when there was no Habitat, no bright and breezy utility, no butchers' aprons or directors' chairs. The style creeps in to every room and is copied ceaselessly but good taste/design is hard to kick even at the challenge of unoriginality. Still very graphic for lighting, bedlinen and kitchenware. Also at 206 Kings Rd, SW3 and King's Mall, Hammersmith, W6.

Heals
196 Tottenham Court Rd, W1 (636 1666)
Mon-Sat 9.00am-5.30.
Furniture of the plain northern kind, good for beds and upholstery and toys. Try their Buzz department in the basement for cheaper and cheerful home ideas.

Laskys
10 Tottenham Court Rd, W1 (637 2232)
Mon-Fri 9.00am-6.00.
Largest branch of the audio hardware shop. Some sharp pricing.

W R Loftus
1/3 Charlotte St, W1 (636 6235)
Mon-Sat 9.00am-5.30, Sat 9.00am-2.30.
Where the amateur distiller goes for advice and the kit. Home-brewing and wine-making.

Nice Irma's Floating Carpet
46 Goodge St, W1 (580 6921)
Mon-Sat 10.00am-6.00.
If you're still into it, this is one of the best Oriental shops for embroideries, wall-hangings, cushions, hand-blocked fabrics and brass lamps.

Reject Shop Houseware
209 Tottenham Court Rd, W1 (637 5567)
Mon-Sat 9.45am-6.00, Thu 9.45am-7.00.
Everything from kitchen equipment to pine at a lesser price than elsewhere as most stock is reject — seconds, ends of lines, samples etc. Reliable source for utility china and glass and tiny presents.

R E W
230 Tottenham Court Rd, W1 (637 2624)
Mon-Sat 9.30am-6.00.
Large video dealers, machines and hire service.

Paperchase
213 Tottenham Court Rd, W1
(580 8496)
Mon-Sat 10.00am-6.00, Thu
10.00am-7.00.
*Paperchase is the city's
stationers. Britain is notorious
for its visual sense but it is
possible to buy cards of wit
and innovation here, together
with writing and wrapping
papers and decorations (the
shop is manic at Christmas).
Upstairs for professional and
specialist papers and inks,
posters and books. Also at 167
Fulham Rd, SW3.*

WHERE TO REST
YOUR FEET

OXFORD ST/REGENT ST'
India Tea Centre
343 Oxford St W1
*The English scone versus the
Indian samosa. East meets
West in the endless variety of
the pot of tea.*

Justin de Blank
54 Duke St, W1
*Cane and zinc and upper home
cooking. Crusty croissants
from J de Bs bakery, French
cheese from his grocery,
graphic salads and excellent
soups.*

Chicago Pizza Pie Factory
17 Hanover Sq, W1
*Where to grab a Schlitz, deep-
dish pizza, loud tables, wooden
floor, video baseball and a nice
day.*

BOND ST
The Granary
39 Albermarle St, W1
*Graphic health food,
casseroles, fresh fruit salads*

*and over the top cakes. Stark
brickwork and flying trays.*

SOUTH MOLTON ST/
ST CHRISTOPHER'S PLACE
Coconut Grove
3 Barrett St, W1
*Trendiburgers and cocktails
like kitsch swimming pools.
Ignore the posing and try the
deep-fried potato skins.*

Widow Appelbaum's
46 South Molton St, W1
*Deli-whizz with wiener
schnitzel, latkes, chicken soup
with matzoballs and Brooklyn
sandwiches mama would
approve of. Take it outside with
an ice-cold beer and watch the
parade go by.*

PICCADILLY
*Piccadilly and St James are
rich in choice. Take a grand
civilised tea at the* **Ritz,**
Piccadilly or **Brown's Hotel,**
Albermarle St. Or:-
Jules Bar
85 Jermyn St, SW1
*Leatherish armchair, waiters
white coat shaking an old-
fashioned cocktail, carpets and
plush.*

Hard Rock Cafe
150 Old Park Lane, W1
*A place that lives up to its
name. Extremely loud and
large hamburgers, crowds and
queues. Shuts up children in no
time.*

The Fountain Bar
Fortnum & Mason, Piccadilly,
SW1
*Greenlight room, gilt chairs,
white tablecloth, large
shopping parcels. China teas,
rarebits, paper-thin*

sandwiches scattered with watercress, and waitress.

SOHO
Maison Bertaux
28 Greek St, W1
Rich French pastry on stark formica. The ancient regime still serve.

Valerie's
44 Old Compton St, W1
Frantic chic. Take the croissant from the basket but not the coffee.

The French House
49 Dean St, W1
Known as the French pub (champagne and beer by the half pint). Soho's haunt of low-life bohemian and hack, throwing back the Pernod.

TOTTENHAM COURT ROAD
Cranks at Heals
196 Tottenham Ct Rd, W1
Good-looking health food blowing hot and cold amongst the furniture. Try muesli topped with molasses for moral strength.

TRANSPORT

(All details subject to change. Phone 01-222 1234 at anytime, day or night to check details. Some routes shown do not operate every day of the week.)

OXFORD STREET (WEST)
Tube: Marble Arch, Bond Street or Oxford Circus
Buses: 1, 2, 2b, 6, 7, 8, 12, 13, 15, 16a, 23, 73, 74, 88, 113, 137, 159, 500, N89, N91, N94.

OXFORD STREET (EAST)
Tube: Oxford Circus or Tottenham Court Road
Buses: 1, 7, 8, 25, 73

REGENT STREET
Tube: Oxford Circus or Piccadilly Circus
Buses: 3, 6, 12, 13, 15, 23, 53, 88, 113, 159, 500, N89, N91, N94

BOND STREET
Tube: Bond Street or Green Park
Buses: 25 or 1, 6, 7, 8, 12, 13, 15, 16a, 23, 73, 88, 113, 137, 159, 500, N89, N91, N94 — to Oxford Street or 9, 14, 22, 38, 55, N97 — to Piccadilly

SOUTH MOLTON ST/ST CHRISTOPHER'S PLACE
Tube: Bond Street
Buses: 1, 6, 7, 8, 12, 13, 15, 16a, 23, 25, 73, 88, 113, 137, 159, 500, N89, N91, N94 — to Oxford Street

PICCADILLY
Tube: Green Park or Piccadilly Circus
Buses: 9, 14, 22, 25, 38, 55, N97

SOHO
Tube: Piccadilly Circus, Leicester Square or Tottenham Court Road
Buses: 1, 7, 8, 25, 73 — to Oxford Street (East) or 1, 14, 19, 22, 24, 29, 38, 55, 176 — to Cambridge Circus

TOTTENHAM COURT ROAD
Tube: Tottenham Court Road, Goodge Street or Warren Street
Buses: 14, 24, 29, 73, 134, 176, N90

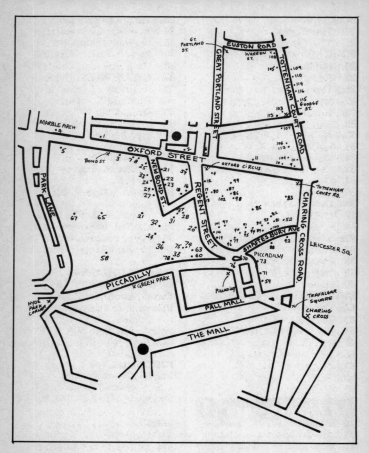

Oxford Street
1. Selfridges
2. John Lewis
3. West One
4. Marks & Spencer
5. Stephen Y
6. Top Shop at Peter Robinson
7. Paris Croissant
8. HMV
9. Virgin Megastore
10. Games Centre
11. Lost Property Sales

Regent Street
12. Liberty's
13. Hamleys
14. Acquascutum
15. Warehouse Utility Clothing Co
16. Roots
17. Jaeger
18. Danish Food Centre
19. Mitsukiku
20. Pencraft

Bond Street
21. Fenwicks
22. The White House
23. Chappell
24. Crolla
25. Elle
26. Fiorucci
27. Ireland House Shop
28. Herbert Johnson
29. Ralph Lauren
30. Anthony Lloyd Jennings
31. Janet Reger
32. Zandra Rhodes
33. The Cocktail Shop
34. Culpeper
35. Smythson
36. Charbonnel & Walker
37. Giddens

Piccadilly & St James
57. Hatchards
58. Heywood Hill
59. Burberrys
60. James Drew
61. Lobbs
62. Locks
63. N Peal
64. Turnbull & Asser
65. John Baily
66. Fortnum & Mason
67. Hobbs
68. Paxton & Whitfield
69. Astleys
70. Boots
71. Design Centre
72. Floris
73. Fribourg & Treyer
74. Irish Linen
75. Sullivan Powell
76. Lillywhites
77. Swaine, Adeney, Briggs & Sons
78. Captain OM Watts

Soho
79. The Vintage Magazine Store
80. Galt Toys
81. P Denny
82. Gamba
83. The Fabric Studio
84. Algerian Coffee Stores
85. Berwick Street and Rupert Street Markets
86. Cranks Helath Foods
87. Cranks Whole Grain Shop
88. Dugdale & Adams
89. Great Wall
90. The House of Floris
91. Lina Stores
92. Loon Fung Supermarket
93. G Parmigiani Figli
94. Randall & Aubin
95. Richards
96. Slater & Cooke, Bisney & Jones
97. Anything Left Handed
98. Craftsmen Potters
99. Harold Moore
100. William Page
101. Stuffed
102. The Yarn Store

Tottenham Court Road
103. Pollock's Toy Museum
104. Ferns
105. Bartholdi
106. Adeptus
107. Byzantium
108. Chivers
109. Habitat
110. Heals
111. Laskys
112. W R Loftus
113. Nice Irma's Floating Carpet
114. Reject Shop Houseware
115. REW
116. Paperchase

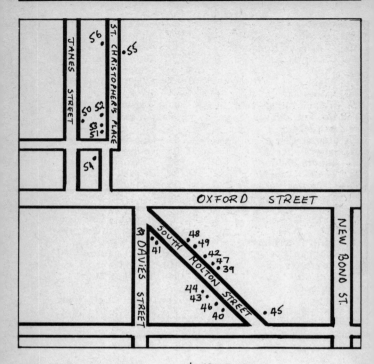

South Molton Street
38. Gray's Antique Market
39. Zero 4
40. Benetton
41. Browns
42. Ebony
43. Joseph
44. Santini e Domenici
45. Monsoon
46. Rider
47. Trussardi

48. Prestat
49. HR Higgins

St Christopher's Place
50. Anastasia
51. Artwork
52. Margaret Howell
53. Mulberry Co
54. Paddy Campbell
55. Teamwork
56. Cutler & Gross

MARYLEBONE & BAYSWATER

DAVID SHILLING

Marylebone, medical village, where the winds of fear blow keenest. Intersected by the traffic-soaked Marylebone Road and the great Northern Stations, Marylebone is a no-man's land; on one side the desolate reaches of Lisson Grove, brightened by Church Street Market, on the other neat bleakness surprised by Marylebone High Street, a ribbon of specialist shops, music shops and windows thick with fashion in an up-market mood.

Bayswater is a twilight zone where the grand houses of the Forsyte Saga between the green edges of Kensington Gardens and the sooty arches of Paddington Station, have crumbled into cheap hotels and bedsits. The main river is Queensway, shiny with all-night neon, supermarkets, foreign newspapers, hamburger bars, junk clothing and the now-darkened windows and pigeon-huddled pillars of Whiteleys, London's first department store.

ANTIQUES

Alfie's Antique Market
13/25 Church St, NW8 (723 6066)
Tue-Sat 10.00am-6.00.
Enclosed space bustling with stalls, bric-a-brac, second-hand books, rural antiques, crates of china and curios, period clothes. Junk junkies rummage the trunk at **Ol' Texas Sells The Past** *at no 30.*

CLOTHES

David Shilling
36 Marylebone High St, W1 (487 3179)
Mon-Fri 9.00am-6.00.
Society's milliner whose couture range cascades 'twixt pale 30s furniture (the ultra couture behind a curtain). Here the hat is the hat (accessory is a forbidden word) a witticism, a point, a sculpture, waiting for the occasion. Bizarre extravagances (mink gloves, silk tea-roses etc) wait in the wings. Know it by the chocolate box window.

Whistles
1 Thayer St, W1 (935 7013)
Mon-Sat 10.00am-6.00.
For the up-market individualist who splashes the style on hand-knit Artwork and reversible Michiko. Also at 20, The Market, Convent Garden, WC2 and 14 Beauchamp Place, SW1. The more mortal price can be found at **Polo** *89 Marylebone High St (don't miss the Chinese footwear)*

FOOD

Church St Market
Church St, W2.
Mon-Sat 9.00am-5.00.
Full market day is on Saturday when the stalls fan out to Lisson Grove. Cheap but noisy fruit and veg plus household linen, kettles, shiny clothes, tools, stuffed toys, shellfish, carpets, cheese and junk.

Clare's Chocolates
3 Park Rd, NW1 (262 1906)
Mon-Sun 9.00am-7.00.
After Regents Park and the Zoo, take a further treat at this superb chocolate shop with over 70 different sweet temptations. Do not resist the truffles.

Druce & Craddock
24 Marylebone High St, W1 (935 3600)
Mon-Fri 7.30am-5.30, Sat 7.30am-3.30.
Good versatile butcher with American and Continental cutting style. Keep a space for the sausages.

The Swedish Shop
7 Paddington St, W1 (486 7077)
Mon-Fri 10.00am-6.00, Sat 9.30am-1.00.
Bleak northern shop glittering with iced glasses. Downstairs for the Bergmanesque — crispbreads, frozen reindeer, Gravad Lax, pickling fluid.

Wholefood Butchers
24 Paddington St, W1 (486 1390)
Mon-Fri 9.00am-6.00, Sat 9.00am-1.00.
At last a health shop for meat

*eaters. Free range butchers —
cold meats, pies, game
(including venison) eggs and
their chickens and the old
carnivore favourites. Also at*
Wholefood *112 Baker St for the
groceries, restaurant and
books of advice.*

HOME

Afia Carpets
81 Baker St, W1 (935 0414)
Mon-Fri 9.00am-5.30, Sat
9.00am-1.00.
*The carpet place. From
coconut matting to the
designer floor, plain to
geometrics. Enormous colour
range and very competitive
pricing.*

John Bell & Croydon
54 Wigmore St, W1 (935 5555)
Mon-Fri 9.00am-6.00, Sat
9.00am-1.00; dispensary Mon-
Sat 8.30am-9.00, Sun
10.00am-8.00.
*Grim with surgical
instruments, wheelchairs and
invalid's aids, this large
respectable pharmacist and
chemist is also well-known for
its long opening hours
especially by the desparate.*

The Button Queen
19 Marylebone Lane, W1 (935
1505)
Mon-Fri 10.00am-5.30, Sat
10.00am-2.30.
*If you've lost your button, you
may well find it here.
Specialists in rare and antique
buttons — metal, horn,
tortoiseshell, ivory, mother of
pearl from party dresses to
greatcoats. Also good for
buckles and cufflinks.*

Distinctive Trimmings
11 Marylebone Lane, W1 (486
6456)
Mon-Fri 9.30am-1.30, 2.30-5.00.
*Braids, brocades, fringes, frills
exclusively for furniture and
curtains. Where to get
Venetian tassels for keys to
desks and harpsichords.*

Divertimenti
68/72 Marylebone Lane, W1
(935 0689)
Mon-Fri 9.30am-6.00, Sat
10.00am-2.00.
*Great kitchen shop,
specialising in French china,
white and utility with brown
glaze stacking cups upstairs,
Provencal flowers and
Mediterranean blue
downstairs. Also for cake tins,
large hearts to tiny aspic
cutters, picnic baskets, shiny
saucepan mountains, shelves
of cookery books plus a knife
sharpening and copper
retinning service.*

BAYSWATER

CLOTHES

Dickie Dirts
58a Westbourne Grove, W2
(229 1466)
Mon-Sun 9.00am-11.00.
*For the cheapest Levis in
town. Scruffy, cramped but
usually worth a fight. Also
good for pioneer checked
shirts etc. Also at 114 Notting
Hill Gate W11; 152 Victoria St,
SW1; Old Cinema,
Camberwell Green.*

FOOD

Athenian Grocery
16a Moscow Rd, W2
(229 6280)
Mon-Sat 9.00am-6.30, Sun
10.00am-1.00.
*Strategically close to the vast
Greek Orthodox church, this
excellent Greek grocer sells
Greek honey, Arab spices,
sesame breads, feta, fresh
herbs, tinned dolmades and
good olives.*

Maison Bouquillon
41/45 Moscow Rd, W2
(727 4897)
Mon-Sat 8.00am-11.00, Sun
8.00am-1.00.
*Very French charcuterie and
patisserie. Salon du the and an
irresistible tarte aux fraises du
bois. Also at 28 Westbourne
Grove, W2.*

Marcus Coffee
13 Connaught St, W2
(723 4020)
Mon-Fri 8.30am-5.30, Sat
8.30am-1.00.
*The sweet smell of roasting
coffee beans drifts about this
rich Bayswater pocket. Thirty
two varieties with machines,
expensive chocolates, esoteric
mustards etc.*

Patisserie Francaise
127 Queensway, W2 (229
0746)
Mon-Sat 10.00am-7.00
*Fine bakery and patisserie
with an old fashioned steamy
window crammed with
endless twists of bread (28)
and cakes (over 100). Tea
rooms at the back. Also at 27
Kensington Church St, W8.*

Peking Store
11 Porchester Rd, W2
(221 4355)
Tue-Sun 10.00am-11.30am, 12
noon-5.30.
*Chinese and health food, teas,
beanshoots, tofu, frozen
Oriental fish, ready-made
dishes such as dumplings and
fish balls, vitamins and woks.*

Thai Shop
3 Craven Terrace, W2 (723
2358)
Mon-Sat 10.00am-7.00,
Sun 12 noon-4.00.
*Exotic and often fearful
looking fruits (including fat
finger bananas, custard apples
and waxy apples) and
vegetables airfreighted from
Bangkok each Friday (the
woven carrier baskets are on
sale outside on the pavement
and makes a thrifty
wastepaper basket). This
friendly shop also sells dried
fish, tinned lychees, Thai silk,
spices and sweets.*

24-Hour Supermarket
68 Westbourne Grove, W2
(727 4927)
*If you're dying for a cigarette,
a pint of milk, a toothbrush,
batteries for the radio,
suddenly and at any time, you
can get it here for a few pence
more. Remember the name.*

HOME

**French Kitchenware And
Tableware Supply Co**
86 Westbourne Grove, W2
(229 5530)
Mon-Fri 9.30am-6.00, Sat
10.00am-5.00.
The trading store for

*Marylebone's Divertimenti.
Enormous saucepans, fish
kettles, moulds etc for
restaurants but still a good
place to seek out Sabatier
knives, pepper grinders,
French white china, Duralex
glass and a great blue jug for
humbler kitchens.*

WHERE TO REST YOUR FEET

Maison Sagne
105 Marylebone High St, W1
*Patisserie and confiserie (don't
miss the kitsch marzipan
flowers). Civilize a grey
hungover morning with a jug
of cafe au lait and croissant and
lose yourself in the amazing
mural of Mediterranean blue,
tumbling rose, Grecian pillar
and spindly palms waving in an
almost imperceptible breeze.
Watch out for artists.*

Maison Bouquillon
4 Moscow Rd, W2
*Marble tops, wrought iron
chairs, croissants and
patisserie. Also at 28
Westbourne Grove, W2.*

TRANSPORT

**(All details subject to change.
Phone 01-222 1234 at anytime,
day or night to check details.
Some routes shown do not
operate every day of the
week.)**

Tube: Bayswater, Queensway,
Paddington,
Marylebone, Edgware
Rd, Baker St
Buses: 1 (Mon-Fri only), 2, 2b,
3, 13, 27, 30, 53, 74,
113, 137 (Mon-Sat,
except evenings), 159,
176 (Mon-Fri only) —
to Marylebone
Or: 7, 12, 15, 23, 27, 36b,
88
Night: N89, N91 — to
Bayswater/Paddington

MARYLEBONE
1. Alfie's Antique Market
2. David Shilling
3. Whistles
4. Church Street Market
5. Clare's Chocolates
6. Druce & Craddock
7. The Swedish Shop
8. Wholefood Butchers
9. Afia Carpets
10. John Bell & Croydon
11. The Button Queen
12. Distinctive Trimmings
13. Divertimenti

BAYSWATER
14. Dickie Dirts
15. Athenian Grocery
16. Maison Bouquillon
17. Marcus Coffee
18. Patisserie Francaise
19. Peking Store
20. Thai Shop
21. 24-hour Supermarket
22. French Kitchenware and
Tableware Supply Co

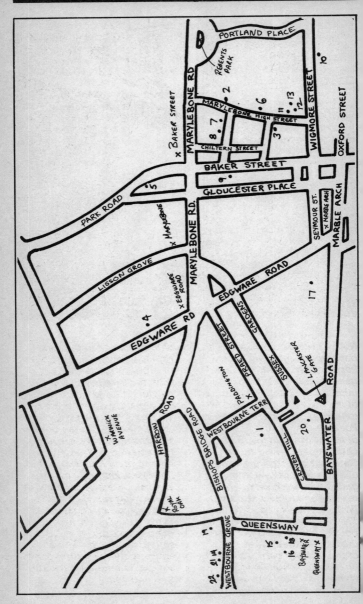

PORTOBELLO MARKET

Notting Hill Gate was always a bad penny, unevenly spun. Peppered with silken-skirted gentleladies upon the Hill inhaling the beneficial fumes of the gravel as it was carted to the city, and workers at the Potteries having little choice of fumes down in the mud-churning Vale, Notting Hill Gate first incurred the wrath of Dickens and Frith and gathered a wickeder reputation on the opening of JW Ladbroke's Hippodrome. The boundaries have never been secured: though many of the fine facades have crumbled and gardens are littered and choked with weed, the grand house and slum still stand together, the wild music of the gypsies replaced by the thicker beat of reggae.

Writers thrive in Notting Hill watching the 'Sturm and Drang' of the pavement from their Georgian creepered windows (politicians prefer the quieter squares of Bayswater and Holland Park). There is a myriad of antique shops that line Westbourne Grove, the Gate and Electric Cinemas at the Notting Hill Carnival to liven every boring summer. Every Saturday Portobello Road erupts into the Market selling much junk, some antiques (though rarely for a song in tuneless days) and fruit and veg.

39

NOTTING HILL & HOLLAND PARK

ANTIQUES

David Black
96 Portland Rd, W11 (727 2566)
Mon-Sat 2.00-6.00.
Specialists in tribal rugs, kelims, soumacs and embroideries, David Black and Clive Loveless also provide a cleaning and restoration service. As the opening times suggest, a very civilised place without that cold superciliousness often encountered in antique shops.

Carries
32 Pembridge Rd, W11 (727 4805)
Mon-Fri 11.00am-5.00, Sat 10.30am-6.00.
Window cluttered charmingly with birdcages, butterflies and butterscotch tins with all the magic of an attic. Inside this Victoriana shop specialises in china and toys, pictures and ephemera. Mr Carries has a great collection of teddy bears and Valentine cards.

Dodo
185 Westbourne Grove, W11 (229 3132)
Tue, Wed, Fri and Sat 12 noon-6.00.
Where the sign is taken seriously. Unfortunately the mass market took the old tin advertising sign and pub mirror and turned it into something cheap and ugly. Here you can buy the originals plus old shop display cases (for chocolate, cigarettes etc) posters, labels, toys and games and a selection of antique clothing.

London Postcard Centre
21 Kensington Park Rd, W11 (229 1888)
Mon-Fri 11.00am-6.00, Sat 9.30-6.30.
The Centre is the headquarters of British antique collection and houses the largest topographical collection in the country. Run by a series of dealers each specialising in different subjects and periods. Amongst the rarer specimens find Ralph Kirschner's gentle erotica, Mucha originals and Fritz Lang's pre-cinematic work. A genuine Hitler Viennese study will set you back several hundreds.

Portobello Market
Portobello Rd, W11.
Sat all day (until dusk in winter)
Antiques Road, shuttered and dark during the week, crowded and frenetic on Saturdays (don't attempt it in a car). Collectors go in the morning and stay in the arcades near the top end. Junk freaks wander down the stall-lined street to the flyover where the hunting begins for second-hand clothes, and bicycles are auctioned from two o'clock.

BOOKS

Elgin Books
6 Elgin Crescent, W11 (229 2186)
Tue-Sat 10.00am-6.00.
Where the Notting Hill group pick up their lit. Know this good small general bookshop (best on fiction and children's books) by the green inside and red awning outside.

Mandarin Books
22 Notting Hill Gate, W11 (229 0327)
Mon-Fri 10.00am-6.30, Sat 10.00am-6.00.
Popular overcrowded book-store. Good for history and politics, well-informed staff who will look in the stock room and order books.

Notting Hill Books
132 Palace Court Gdns, W8 (727 5988)
Mon-Sat 10.00am-6.00.
A haven for remaindered and review copies, especially for art and lit crit. Outside a stall for addicts of old Penguins.

CHILDREN

Mother's Ruin
126 Holland Park Rd, W11 (727 1116)
Mon-Sat 9.30am-5.00.
More to do with expense than gin. Mother's Ruin have children's clothes from the achingly nostalgic sailor suits and smocked dresses to tough French cords and English duffle coats for those who prefer to climb trees. There is also a selection of illustrated books and Galt toys to quell the fractious whilst the grown-ups decide.

Tigermoth
166 Portobello Rd, W11 (727 7564)
Mon-Sat 9.30-5.30.
Tigermoth is for children of the dungaree generation. Neither shops party or supermarket the shops are strong on bright, practical clothes — jewel-coloured velour from Sweden, woollen tights and Arran hand knits. Plus Petit Bateau underwear, lunchboxes and pocket money toys.

CLOTHES

John Burke
20 Pembridge Rd, W11 (229 0862)
Mon-Fri 9.00am-5.00.
Lined with shelves of antiquarian books and sunk in Forsthian gloom, John Burke keep fine dress suits and cavalry uniforms at the back. Be tempted first by the window where shiny toppers, white gloves and coloured cummerbunds wait quietly for a night at the opera.

Hindukush
231 Portobello Rd, W1 (727 4865)
Mon-Sat 10.00am-6.00.
Modern ethnics (as opposed to the meagre cheesecloth and committed kaftan). Rich tartans, lurex streaked harem pants and a great selection of Madras scarves.

Kickself
188 Portobello Rd, W11 (221 1084)
Seven days a week, 10.00am-8.00.
Efficient shoe supermarket with cut-price feet under £20. Mostly Kickers, redoubtable French boots, baseball boots and a few labels like Walkers. Good for pavement-scuffing kids.

Renegade
186 Kensington Park Rd, W11
(221 7354)
Mon-Sat 9.30am-6.00.
Sharp cut leather clothes, best for jackets.

FOOD

Ceres Bakery
269a Portobello Rd, W11 (229 5571)
Mon-Sat 10.00am-6.00.
Bakery of the wholegrain kind, plus herbs, organics and yoghurts of many varieties. The home baked pies are delicious.

Delices des Gascogne
3 Hillgate St, W8 (221 4131)
Mon-Sat 10.00am-9.30.
Bricked and tiled a la Provencale, this gourmet shop tempts with rows of wild boar terrines, hare pates, lobster bisques and baskets of crusty loaves for the ultimate picnic; quenelles of pike, cassoulet with preserved goose and pigeon casseroled in red wine for the candle-flickered night. Hampers are packed for delicious presents.

C Lidgate
10 Holland Park Ave, W11 (727 8243)
Mon-Fri 7.30am-6.00, Sat 7.30am-5.00.
Edwardian butcher, tiles and mahogany pay desk. Excellent meat, fresh poultry, game, gateaux, delicious sausages, pastries and pies, French and English cheeses, home made jams and chutneys and a devilish petit pot au chocolat.

Mr Christian's
11 Elgin Crescent, W11 (229 0501)
Mon-Fri 9.00am-7.00, Sat 9.00am-6.00, Sun 9.30am-2.00.
Popular well-stocked delicatessen with wide range of cheese, pies, home-made meatballs etc.

Quality Delicatessen Stores
133a Notting Hall Gate, W11 (229 3689)
Mon-Sat 9.45am-7.00.
Good Polish delicatessen, known as Salik's and famous and ripe decadent Brie, sausage and dark mittel-European breads.

HOME

Bedlam
130 Notting Hill Gate, W11 (229 5360)
Mon-Sat 10.00am-6.00, Thu 10.00am-8.00.
The utility wooden bed, mattresses and bedlinen with some stripey nightshirts and caps.

Between The Sheets
190 Kensington Park Rd, W11 (727 8768)
Mon-Sat 10.00am-6.00.
Sheets, cushions, quilts, nightshirt cases etc in American percale, striped, patterned and plain.

Bland and Son
24b Notting Hill Gate, W11 (229 6711)
Mon-Sat 9.00am-6.00.
Bland advertise their existence in the old way, large letters on the side of a building and a metal cut-out umbrella.

Umbrellas and luggage both sold and repaired.

Buyers & Sellers
120/122 Ladbroke Grove, W11 (229 1947)
Mon-Sat 9.00am-5.00, Thu 9.00am-12 noon.
Whizz kids of the white goods trade, Buyers & Sellers seem to undercut every other discount fridge, freezer and washing machine. There may be a slight knock on the outside but the mechanics come with a guarantee.

Graham & Green
4 & 7 Elgin Crescent, W11 (727 4594)
Mon-Sat 9.30am-6.00.
No 4 is full of practicality: kitchenware, basket ware, fresh potted herbs from April, birthday cake tins for hire, always good for plain French china; no 7 'Over The Road' is full of prettiness, presents of fruit china, spotted glass, walking canes, white appliqued tablecloths, gift wrapped food and cane downstairs.

John Oliver
33 Pembridge Rd, W11 (727 3735)
Mon-Sat 10.00am-6.00.
The wallpaper shop. Here latterday William Morris may have his own designs printed on paper, foil or vinyl and any paint colour will be mixed in emulsion in four to five days. John Oliver will also hand print his own designs in any specific colour in 10 to 14 days... pastel clouds to Marilyn Monroe.

Virginia
98 Portland Rd, W11 (727 2566)
Mon-Sat 2.00-6.00.
Wide variety of Victorian and 30s kitchen and bathroom furniture. Baths for hiding in on bad mornings with brass taps, French enamel stoves, lace curtains, pine shutters and Gothic clothing.

WHERE TO REST YOUR FEET

Geales Fish Restaurant
2/4 Farmer St, W8
Parlour tea and fish shop. Take it fresh, plain and battered with lots of tartar peas and wine.

Julie's Bar
37 Portland Rd, W11
Palm dark interior, carved wood, rich sofas and Gothic cakes to match — take one of these with a glass of cold wine on a late depressed afternoon. Does wonders for melancholia.

Obelix
294 Westbourne Grove, W11
Buckwheat gallettes, rough cider, blackboard, floorboard, papers. Eating in a paved garden for summer optimists.

TRANSPORT

(All details subject to change. Phone 01-222 1234 at anytime, day or night to check details. Some routes shown do not operate every day of the week.)

Tube: Notting Hill Gate, Holland Park, Ladbroke Grove

Buses: 7, 12, 15, 23, 27, 28, 31, 52, 52a, 88 **Night:** N89

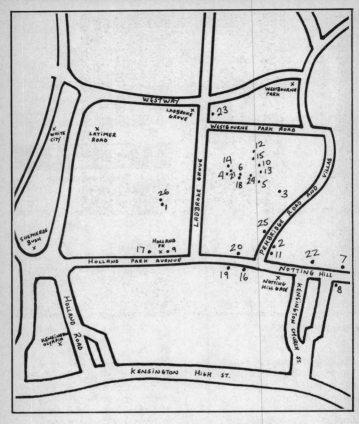

1.	David Black	15.	Ceres Bakery
2.	Carries	16.	Delices des Gascogne
3.	Dodo	17.	C Lidgate
4.	London Postcard Centre	18.	Mr Christian's
5.	Portobello Market	19.	Quality Delicatessen
6.	Elgin Books		Stores
7.	Mandarin Books	20.	Bedlam
8.	Notting Hill Books	21.	Between the Sheets
9.	Mothers Ruin	22.	Bland & Son
10.	Tigermoth	23.	Buyers & Sellers
11.	John Burke	24.	Graham & Green
12.	Hindukush	25.	John Oliver
13.	Kickself	26.	Virginia
14.	Renegade		

KENSINGTON

ANTHONY SELTON

Kensington was ever genteel. The quiet shady square, the nannies in the Gardens, the pubs that sell more Campari than beer. Once when the boutique was queen, the news was that Kensington High Street was to be the place after the King's Road. It never made it. Maybe because the reign ended. Maybe because Kensington was just too respectable, lacking Chelsea's careless bohemianism. The High Street was once dominated by three giant facades: Derry & Toms, Pontings and Barkers: now only Barkers remains. The crowds have fled the old department stores and are to be found in the shiny multi-purpose King's Mall Shopping Centre in Hammersmith (Habitat Mothercare etc). The 'ancien régime' takes a stroll down Kensington Church Street, slowly, for Ming and things.

CENTRES

Barkers
Kensington High St, W8 (937 5432)
Mon-Wed and Fri 9.00am-5.30, Tue 9.30am-5.30, Thu 9.00am-7.00, Sat 9.00am-6.00.
Last of the Kensington department stores, Barkers is useful for most things but outstanding for nothing. Best on practicality, haberdashery, electricals and children's clothes.

ANTIQUES

Antique Hypermarket
26 Kensington High St, W8 (937 3727)
Mon-Sat 10.00am-5.45.
Indoor antique market with over a 100 stalls selling mainly decorative pieces, especially clocks, jewellery and old dolls.

Anthony Belton
14 Holland St, W8 (937 1012)
Mon-Sat 10.00am-6.00, closed between 1.00-2.00.
Eclectic collector of the decorative: excellent ceramics (especially English Delft), tapestries, primitive paintings. Great for teapots for those with an expansive sense of humour.

John Jesse & Irina Laski
160 Kensington Church St, W8 (229 0312)
Mon-Sat 10.00am-6.00.
Delicious Art Deco and Art Nouveau shop, furniture to Lalique glass. Specialises in accessories such as handbags and plastic jewellery.

The Lacquer Chest
75 Kensington High St, W8 (937 1306)
Mon-Fri 9.30am-5.30, Sat 9.30am-1.30.
Ablaze with roaring winter fire and charm, this antique shop appears as a cluttered drawing room. China, carpets, brass light switches, mirrors for the perfect hallway, quilts and bizarre 'practical' items such as an American hair-restoring machine. Good for presents.

Maureen Thompson
34 Kensington Church St, W8 (937 9919)
Mon-Fri 10.00am-1.00, 2.00-5.00, Sat 10.30am-4.30.
Specialist in 18th Century drinking glass for those who take their claret in style. Also Victorian coloured glass and decanters.

BOOKS

Children's World
229 Kensington High St, W8 (937 6314)
Mon-Sat 9.30am-6.00.
Fiction, encyclopaedias, books in foreign languages, picture books, everything tiny book worms want. Plus large selection of party toys, masks, jokes and dressing up clothes.

Kensington Bookshop
140 Kensington Church St, W8 (727 0544)
Mon-Fri 10.00am-6.00, Sat 10.00am-5.30.
Good general bookshop with an emphasis on children's books and a dynamic range of cards and wrapping paper.

Studio Bookshop
123 Kensington Church St, W8
(727 4995)
Tue-Sat 10.00am-6.00.
A classic of second-hand bookshops. Cluttered, well informed, good for remaindered stock, catalogues and art books.

CHILDREN

Anthea Moore Ede
16 Victoria Grove, W8 (584 8826)
Mon-Fri 9.00am-5.00, Sat 10.00am-1.00.
The perfect clothes for that endless Edwardian summer: white drill sailor suits, Liberty print shirts, hand-smocked dresses. Where to go for children's fancy dress, polka dot clowns, Red Indians, star-spangled fairies etc. Complete nursery service — cradles to knitted bootees.

Pom
47 Kensington Church St, W8
(937 8641)
Mon-Sat 10.00am-5.00.
Small French clothes shop with English knits, traditional shoes and ribbed tights.

Tree House
237 Kensington High St, W8
(937 7497)
Mon-Sat 9.30am-5.30.
Once one of the more innovative toy shops in London, the Tree House has now switched the image and become a party shop (stationery, paper plates, prizes, hire of tables etc). Soda bar for bright sickly concoctions and a real bath to try out the bath toys.

CLOTHES

Benetton
129/131 Kensington High St,
W8 (937 3034)
Mon-Sat 10.00am-6.30, Thu 10.00am-7.00.
Modern Italian knitwear in all the colours of the woolly rainbow, plain corduroy and soft kilts. O12 at no 131 is Benetton for kids. Also at 6 South Molton St, W1; 40 Hampstead High St, NW3.

Hennes
High St Kensington Shopping Precinct, W8 (937 7825)
Mon-Fri 9.30am-6.30, Thu 9.30am-7.00, Sat 9.30am-6.00.
Scandinavian plain cut clothes. Best for children downstairs, stripey short sets, track suits and classic pleated skirts.

Kensington Market
Kensington High St, W8.
Mon- Sat 10.00am-5.30.
Battle through the cut price jeans and afghans (those still left over and some now there self-consciously) and grab the ephemeral street fashion. Whatever your retro beat, you will find it here: rockabilly, punk, psychedelia, 60s plastic, Hollywood glamour. Still good for second-hand stalwarts like crombies, dinner suits, military jackets, 30s flower cotton dresses, scarves and braces.

Meenys
197 Kensington High St, W8
(938 7899)
Mon-Sat 10.00am-6.00.
American hamburger and baseball style: sweatshirts,

47

bakers' and painters' trousers, tracksuits, caps, rainbow braces, jeans and dungarees from 9 months.

Patricia Roberts
1b Kensington Church Walk, W8 (937 0097)
Mon-Sat 10.00am-6.00.
Wool shop. Every natural fibre in every living colour and one of the few places to stock 100 per cent mohair. Rough wholemeal, rainbow stripes, fluffy pastels, clack the needles to Patricia Robert's annual knitting book. The finished originals are expensive — lazybones have to pay.

Roxy
25 Kensington Church St, W8 (937 2523)
Mon-Fri 10.00am-6.00, Thu 10.00am-7.00, Sat 10.00am-6.30.
Up-style on two floors. Fresh silks from Charlotte Flood, and Jasper Conran, shirts by Fenn Wright & Manson, leather jackets and belts.

Slick Willies
47 Kensington High St, W8 (937 9547)
Mon-Sat 9.30am-6.00.
American sportswear always dashing on the latest craze. Once skateboards, now catering for roller skaters on the wane and CB radios. Take the gear here for baseball, ice-hockey, roller-hockey, American football, volley and basketball.

Tomlinson & Tomlinson
8 Hornton Rd, W8 (937 5173)
Mon-Fri 10.00am-6.00, Thu 10.00am-7.00am, Sat 10.00am-5.30.

Scarecrow arms wave the decade's moving art form, the designer knit. Labels include Warm & Wonderful, Vanessa Keegan, Maggie White and Sasha Kagan. Traditionalists forego the animals and graffiti and wear jumpers for urban fisher-persons: Guernseys, Ganseys, Hebridean, Hanois and Shetland. Sister shop to **The Scottish Merchant,** *16 New Row, WC2.*

Vanilla
35 Kensington Church St, W8 (937 7030)
Mon-Sat 10.00am-6.00.
Party shop. Rich tiers, glitter and theatrical gold. Most clothes are made with their own prints from the workshops downstairs. Good for geometric T-shirt sundresses. Also at 26 Wellington St, WC2.

FOOD

Shepherds Bush Market
Goldhawk Rd, W12.
Mon-Sat 9.00am-5.00, Thu 9.00am-1.00.
Set behind the BBC studios beneath the railway arches this market is wild with African and West Indian specialist foodstuffs, especially fruit and veg, plus cheap fabrics, pet food, hats, plants and all the jostling chaos of the cobbled street.

HOME

Animal Fair
17 Abingdon Rd, W8 (937 0011)
Mon-Sat 9.30am-6.00.

Glass windows bounce with small balls of canine and feline fluff to melt the chocolate hearts. Where the pampered pet gets his bed and frozen foods. The staff are specially trained in pet care and are always extremely helpful. Animal Fair also stock tropical and marine fish, white mice and birds and will board any animal (including budgerigars).

Crabtree & Evelyn
6, Kensington Church St, W8 (997 9335)
Mon-Sat 9.30am-6.00.
There is a land where we all ache to live: a land where time sits under a chestnut tree in a summer's afternoon and watches a child in white bowl a hoop across a wide clipped lawn; a land of correspondences, fresh milk and noble feelings. Pretending to be there, we substitute in the real world, pine dressers for modern sideboards, collect tins and have Beatrix Potter and the Diary of an Edwardian country lady in the bookshelves. Crabtree & Evelyn realised the seductive charms of the nostalgia package years ago and are rarely bettered. Everything from Tudor Guest Soaps to Highland shortbread, incorporating French preserves, green olive oil, salt, shampoo, fudge and herbs. The best labels in the city. Difficult to resist even in the face of reality.

Dilemma
22 Thackeray St, W8 (937 9059)
Mon-Sat 10.00am-6.00.
Wacky gift shop with the inevitable tin toys, ceramics, clocks and stationery. Where to go to find your light up Mr Michelin man.

Strangeways
3 Holland St, W8 (937 3251)
Mon-Sat 10.00am-6.00.
The original Strangeways shop selling clocks, lighting, mirrors and other graphic stuff midway between the quirk and the amazing imagination. Also at 19 The Market, Covent Garden, WC2.

Video Palace
62/64 Kensington High St, W8 (937 8587)
Mon-Fri 10.00am-8.00, Sat 9.30am-6.00.
Where the video kooks rent the system. Huge stocks of pre-recorded tapes, plus home computers, CB radio, satellite dishes and posters.

The Scarsdale Arms
23a Edwardes Sq, W8
Summer evenings outside on the pavement, winter nights by the blazing fire. Where the Guernseys and Green Wellies meet for gin and food of the quicher kind. This square is one of the most enviable in London.

Daquise
20 Thurloe St, SW7
Polish cafe. Go here for lemon tea and borscht.

Maison Verlon
12 Bute St, SW7
Old fashioned tea room wild with French and Austrian pâtisserie.

TRANSPORT

(**All details subject to change. Phone 01-222 1234 at anytime, day or night to check details. Some routes shown do not operate every day of the week.**)

Tube: High Street Kensington, South Kensington, Notting Hill Gate
Buses: 9, 27, 28, 31, 33 (Mon-Sat only, but not evening), 49, 52, 52a — to Kensington High St
Or 14, 30, 45, 49, 74 — to South Kensington

1. Barkers
2. Antique Hypermarket
3. Anthony Belton
4. John Jesse & Irina Laski
5. The Lacquer Chest
8. Kensington Bookshop
9. Studio Bookshop
10. Anthea Moore Ede
11. Pom
12. Tree House
13. Benetton
14. Hennes
15. Kensington Market
16. Meenys
17. Patricia Roberts
18. Roxy
19. Slick Willies
20. Tomlinson & Tomlinson
21. Vanilla
22. Shepherd's Bush Market
23. Animal Fair
24. Crabtree & Evelyn
25. Dilemma
26. Strangeways
27. Video Palace

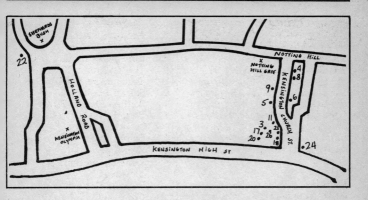

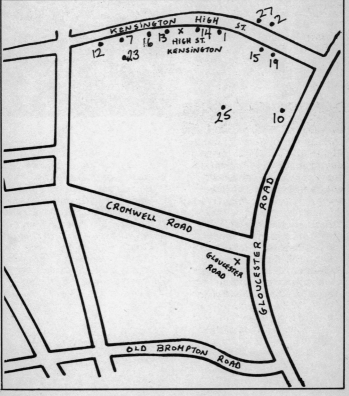

FULHAM

THE. KILN

The Fulham Road goes
further than you think. It
leads to Fulham Town, a
quiet suburban place invaded
by the urban gentry, their
divorces, bottles of Chianti
and Yucca plants. Fulham is
an intrepid stalk for a
shopper but one worth the
pavement-grind since it is
rich in furniture and antique
shops. At the end of King's
Road over the bridge find the
more expensive items,
Wandsworth Bridge Road a
mecca of pine, and Dawes,
Lillie and Munster Roads for
junk. Before you step out one
bright blue day, turn first into
Brompton Cemetery, one of
the calmest places in London,
where even the buses are
drowned in the birdsong
quiet.

ANTIQUES

Barrie Quinn
1 & 3 Broxholme House, New King's Rd, SW10 (736 4747)
Mon-Sat 10.00am-5.30.
One part of Barrie Quinn is devoted to antiques, the other to the jardinière, large ornate colour streaked vases for plants. Make sure you have a grand house to put it in first.

CHILDREN

The Doll's Hospital
16 Dawes Rd, SW6 (385 2081)
Mon-Sat 9.30am-5.30, closed Thu.
Old toyshop that mends the victims of childhood tantrums especially those that took place in Victorian and Edwardian nurseries. Blind and legless teddies also seen to.

Patricks
107/111 Dawes Rd, SW6 (385 9864)
Mon-Sat 9.00am-5.30, Sun 9.00am-1.00.
General toyshop, specialising in model railways (all leading names and accessories) and models, particularly Airfix.

Pierrot
174 Wandsworth Bridge Rd, SW6 (736 1123)
Mon-Sat 10.00am-6.00, Thu 10.00am-1.00.
Imaginative place alive with painted furniture (personalised by commission), hand made cradles, wooden puzzles, party dresses made from Victorian lace and pale silk sashes and speed bright track-suits.

Pollyanna
811 Fulham Rd, SW6 (731 0674)
Mon-Sat 9.30am-5.30.
Principally for the mail order (write to 660 Fulham Rd). Pollyanna sell playground practicality at competitive prices. Boiler suits, swimwear, striped pyjamas, gingham pinafores, sunhats, T-shirts and track-suits in strong colours and no fuss.

The Singing Tree
69 New King's Rd, SW10 (736 4527)
Mon-Sat 10.00am-5.30, Thu 10.00am-1.00.
Everything for the respectable doll's house from real silver trays to hand painted books. Most of the items are for the grown up collector but there are pocket-money miniatures. Ready made houses plus all the accessories for the tiny DIY enthusiast, including a range of copied Victorian wallpapers.

CLOTHES

Kickback
156/8 Wandsworth Bridge Rd, SW6 (736 3115)
Mon-Fri 10.00am-6.00, Thu 10.00am-7.00, Sat 10.00am-4.00.
London's first shoe supermarket selling the French boot and other Kicker shoes from discontinued lines, samples and slightly damaged stock. Good for utility feet.

Lunn Antiques
86 New King's Rd, SW6 (736 4638)
Mon-Sat 10.00am-6.30.

A lost world of white lace and starched cotton. Linen for the house — damask tablecloths, huge ribboned square pillows, drifting curtains; clothes for the nostalgic, peach silk for dressing gowns, christening robes, children's party dresses and the finest lace blouses, especially Edwardian high- necks, in the city.

Van der Fransen
96 Waterford Rd, SW6 (736 3814)
Tue-Sat 10.00am-6.00.
Period clothes for women, especially for the beaded flapper dresses of the 20s.

FOOD

Buy Late Foods
99 Hammersmith Rd, W14 (603 2300)
Mon-Sun 9.00am-10.00.
Remember the name if you're in the area and need last minute milk, aspirins, cigarettes etc.

Old Brompton Colonial
255 Old Brompton Rd, SW10 (373 9131)
Mon-Sun 9.00am-10.00.
Good general delicatessen.

Robert Troop
151 Earl's Court Rd, SW5 (370 1020)
Mon-Sat 8.30am-6.00.
This master baker has a window of sticky and Chelsea buns, hot slices of quiche, sausage rolls to take away, Justin de Blank sausages, pasties and good brown bread.

Leatham's Larder
51 Hollywood Rd, SW10 (351 1053)
Mon-Fri 10.00am-8.00, Sat 10.00am-5.30.
'Purveyors of fine foods and wines' Leatham's sell delicious smoked fish (salmon to trout pate), frozen sea foods (Greenland prawns to Alaskan crab claws), game (venison mince to snipe), poultry, quails' eggs, sucking pig, charcuterie, Stiltons, dried mushrooms, variety of French vinegars and walnut oil.

Luigi's
60 New King's Rd, SW6 (731 4994)
Mon-Sat 10.00am-9.00, Sun 12 noon-2.00.
Bright red facade, inside high shelves shiny with tins, pasta, olive oils and multifarious Italian wines. Good for taking away home-made salads, cold meats, pates and cheesecake.

North End Road Market
North End Road, SW6.
Mon-Sat 9.00am-5.00, Sun 9.00am-1.00.
Catch the fresh fruit, veg, fish and dairy products here at sharp prices.

HOME

And So To Bed
7 New King's Rd, SW10 (731 3593)
Mon-Sat 10.00am-6.00.
And So To Bed is for those who think there is more to a bed than a mere divan and duvet. Specialists in the iron and brass bed, this shop sells antique and reproduction

versions. The iron and brass originals start at about £125 but can veer into thousands. Utter nostalgics can then go the whole hog and accessorise with the Victorian linen, patchwork quilts and huge square pillows filled with duck down. Also at 96b Camden High St, NW1.

Beggars Banquet
8 Hogarth Rd, SW5 (370 6175)
Mon-Sat 10.00am-7.00.
Lively stocked record and tape shop with wide range of styles from classical to reggae. Buy and sell second-hand records and take part-exchange.

Barnums
67 Hammersmith Rd, W14 (602 1211)
Mon-Fri 9.00am-5.00, Sat 10.00am-4.00.
Party palace. The 'Carnival Novelties' include masks, Father Christmas costumes, makeup, wigs and beards, streamers, trimmings, ballons, party hats, paper lanterns and false noses. Hire a marquee here.

Brats
624c Fulham Rd, SW10 (731 6915)
Mon-Sat 10.00am-6.00.
Great adult toyshop. Painted mugs, American tin cars and toy robots, knickerbocker glory glasses, best of the modern stationery (including the Fiorucci range), plastic jewellery, graphic briefcases, coloured socks, Zippo lighters etc. If you're stuck for present ideas, be spoilt here. Also at **Brats Stationery,** Fulham Broadway Arcade, SW10.

Furniture Cave
533 King's Rd, SW10 (351 3870)
Mon-Sat 10.00am-6.00.
Four floors and over 100 stalls sell furniture from the English countryside, 18th Century town houses, giant Victorian pieces and wrought iron staircases. The range is as vast as the space.

Fulham Pottery
210 New King's Rd, SW6 (731 2167)
Mon-Fri 9.00am-5.00, Sat 9.00am-12 noon.
Founded in 1671 by the legendary potter John Dwight, the first to manufacture stoneware on a commercial scale in this country. The original kiln still stands, though surrounded by office monstrosity. Erstwhile de Morgans may buy all the necessary equipment and materials here, tools, differing clays and kilns.

Garden Crafts
158 New King's Rd, SW6 (736 1615)
Mon-Fri 9.00am-6.00, Sat 10.00am-3.00.
Contemplate your own Grecian urn here where a paved zone is crazy with wrought iron garden furniture, statues, zany-eyed toads, sphinxes, sundials, water-spouting gorgons and palms.

Gilded Lily
293 Lillie Rd, SW6 (385 6153)
Mon-Sat 10.00am-6.00.
Bizarre mixture of modern ceramics and cards, Art Deco solid china pieces, bronze lamps and basket chairs. Best

curtains, geometric carpets and tea sets.

Just Sofas
216 New King's Rd, SW10 (731 5606)
Mon-Fri 9.30am-5.00, closed 1.00-2.30, Sat 11.00am-5.00.
They do sell a few cottage chairs but the main song is the sofa, upright, traditional Knole, Chesterfield, sometimes modern with the odd sofa bed. The stock changes quite a bit so it is worth ringing them up beforehand to check what is available. The sofas come in varying states of repair but upholsterers and repairers are recommended and missing feather cushions can be ordered.

Merchant Chandler
72 New King's Rd, SW6 (736 6141)
Mon-Fri 9.30am-5.30, Thu 8.45am-1.30.
Three floors of relentless home utility: baskets of cutlery, wooden pegs, white china, baskets, cane, straw matting, blinds, glass, bamboo and wooden furniture.

Naylor's
131 Munster Rd, SW6 (731 3679)
Mon-Fri 10.00am-6.00, Sat 10.30am-4.45, closed Thu.
Junk fiends' delight. Coloured china, large stocks of tins, tablecloths, old clothes, radios, mirrors etc.

Shop For Painted Furniture
95 Waterford Rd, SW6 (736 1908)
Tue-Sat 10.00am-6.00.
Wooden furniture decorated

to design or to your commission, traditional Gretel to animals.

Pine Mine
100 Wandsworth Bridge Rd, SW10 (736 1092)
Mon-Fri 10.00am, Sat 10.00am-4.30.
Wandsworth Bridge Road was once famed for its eel pie and mash shop, now it's overrun by pine shops. Here you cannot see the wood for the dressers, chests of drawers, cupboards and kitchen tables. Architectural items such as doors with stained glass, staircases, fireplaces with tiles find further down the road at no 318.

Rassells
80 Earl's Court Rd, W8 (937 0481) Mon-Sat 9.00am- 5.30, Thu 9.00am-6.30.
Excellent nursery: equipment, vegetables, terracotta pots, herbaceous borders, seeds, cut flowers, unusual plants. Often beleaguered with the bed-sit mob grabbing house plants to brighten their rooms.

Resista Carpets
255 New King's Rd, SW6 (731 2588)
Mon-Sat 9.00am-6.00.
Home of the tough carpet at a good price. Personal service.

Second Hand City
North End Rd, W14 (385 7711)
Mon-Sat 10.00am-6.15.
Once a Methodist Church, the crypt has now become a basement crammed with second-hand furniture, likewise the nave. The stock is usually modern, quite ugly but

well-priced. Apart from chests of drawers, mirrors etc there is a good supply of used cookers, mattresses and crockery.

Sitting Pretty
131 Dawes Rd, SW6
(381 0049)
Mon-Fri 9.30am-5.30, closed between 1.00-2.00.
Sitting Pretty are renowned for their reproduction wooden lavatory seats (decorated or plain) but also have an antique bathroom section which sells Victorian and Edwardian loos, cast iron baths, all claw feet and brass taps, basins, from the shell soap sort to square deco versions and a good selection of bathroom tiles.

Sophistocat
192 Wandsworth Bridge Rd, SW6 (731 2221)
Mon-Fri 10.00am-6.00, Sat 10.00am-5.00.
Pine is going back to the paint but for those who still take it stripped, watch for that wood plunged into caustic soda which gives it a dull, dead sheen. This is one shop that still sands its furniture. Mostly made to order, principally from old floor joists.

Tile Reject Shop
178 Wandsworth Bridge Rd, SW6 (731 6098)
Mon-Fri 9.30am-5.30, Sat 9.30am-5.00.
Selection of different designs for floor and wall, plain and coloured, mostly British with Italianate exceptions. Rejects are usually due to variations in glaze or tone rather than breaks.

Whiteway & Waldron
305 Munster Rd, SW6 (381 3195)
Mon-Fri 10.00am-6.00, Sat by appointment only.
Here the relics of the past domestic and ecclesiastical, sit torn from their original gloom. Architectural fittings and stained glass from churches and houses are restored and sold — pews, doors, fire surrounds, balustrades mostly in Victorian wood.

Christopher Wray's Lighting Emporium
600/602 New King's Rd, SW6 (736 8008/5989)
Mon-Sat 10.00am-6.00.
Christopher Wray trips the light fantastic and takes most of this part of New King's Road to himself. Notice it by the large clock and window brilliant with decorative lighting of 1880s to 1920s. Most of the stock is copied from original lamps, using old tools from closed factories in solid brass and hand-blown glass. Brackets and shades. Also at **Christopher Wray's Tiffany Shop,** *no 593;* **Christopher Wray's Pot Shop** *no 606 and* **Terracotta Pots** *no 591;* **Christopher Wray's Lamp Workshop** *(for spare parts) no 613.*

FULHAM

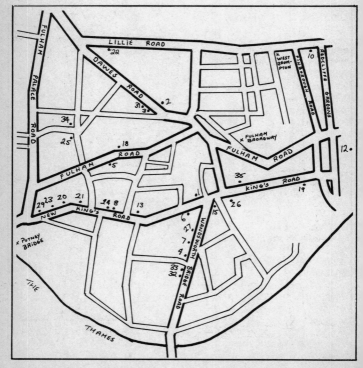

FULHAM

TRANSPORT

Crocodile Tears
660 Fulham Rd, SW6
There is a beast to justify the name and a wine list to provoke a smile (see blackboard for bargains). Food of bistro variety, including crudites, goulash and burgers

Carlos and Johnnys
268 Fulham Rd, SW10
Large ostensibly New York singles bar — cocktails and chillis on the tables, bears and aeroplanes suspended from the ceiling.

(All details subject to change. Phone 01-222 1234 at anytime, day or night to check details. Some routes shown do not operate every day of the week.)

Tube: Fulham Broadway, Putney Bridge, West Kensington, Parsons Green

Buses: 11, 14, 22, 28, 30, 31, 74, 91 (Mon-Sat only), 220, 295

Night: N97

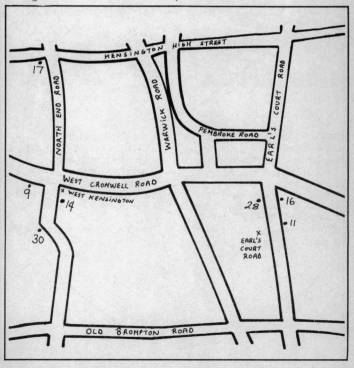

CHELSEA

JOHNSON'S

Chelsea was once the haunt of the haute bohemian. Scored by three highways of Fulham Road, King's Road and the grey glittering Thames, the houses are now too rare a price to cage any garret birds. King's Road though grown tarnished from its golden swinging days when the boutique was bountiful still prances with 'street fashion' every Saturday. Cut the cloth at **P W Forte, Pinto, Jones** and catch the latest bandwagon at **Vivienne Westwood's** World's End, she who brought the pirate on to dry land.

FULHAM ROAD

BOOKS

Pan Bookshop
158 Fulham Rd, SW10 (373 4997)
Mon-Sat 10.00am-10.30, Sun 2.30-6.30.
London's late-night bookshop. All the Pans in print plus a large range of other paperbacks, media and children's books.

CHILDREN

Chelsea Design Co
65 Sydney St, SW3 (352 4626)
Mon-Sat 10.00am-6.00.
Sailor suits, navy blue or striped (also for grown-ups), Liberty print hand-smocked dresses, silk for parties, cord and tough check for pavements, satin ballet shoes and straw hats. Almost everything is designed in-house.

CLOTHES

Laura Ashley
157 Fulham Rd, SW3 (584 6939)
Mon-Fri 9.30am-6.00, Wed 9.30am-7.00, Sat 10.00am-5.30.
Relentless throwing of flowers over wallpapers, smocks, materials. No matter how you view the bucolic charm, Laura Ashley are always excellent for crisp white governess shirts and nightdresses, and theatrically inspired cotton clothes. One of the first places to promote nostalgic fashion in the 70s.

Brother Sun
171 Fulham Rd, SW3 (589 6180)
Mon-Sat 10.00am-6.00.
Fresh Provencal cottons in colours of baked earth, sun red and hot sky blue made in baggy shorts, umbrellas and bags. Where to buy the espadrilles out of season.

Butler & Wilson
189 Fulham Rd, SW3 (352 2045)
Mon-Sat 10.00am-6.00.
Art Deco freakettes go here to buy the real thing or the version inspired. Mainline jewellery plus boxes, cigarette cases and over the top old spectacles. Also at Liberty's.

Great Expectations
46 Fulham Rd, SW3 (584 3468)
Mon-Fri 10.00am-5.30, Sat 10.30am-5.00.
Sited in a bygone glass flower house and a-bloom with designer maternity wear, especially for formal occasions and the beach. Plus Paul Howie dungarees and knitted cushions for the new-born in sampler style by commission.

Night Owls
78 Fulham Rd, SW3 (584 2451)
Mon-Sat 10.00am-6.00.
American nightwear, embroidered white to T-shirt stripe.

Piero Di Monzi
68 Fulham Rd, SW3 (589 8765)
Mon-Sat 10.00am-5.30

Low-key Italian clothes, strong fabrics, structured style. For men and women. Often Cerruti, always expensive.

Tatters
74 Fulham Rd, SW3 (584 1532)
Mon-Fri 10.00am-6.00, Sat 10.00am-5.00.
Romantic frills and old lace for the nostalgic ball or wedding.

FOOD

Hundred Acre Farm Shop
51 Hollywood Rd, SW10 (351 1053)
Mon-Fri 10.00am-6.00, Sat 9.00am-5.00.
Fine frozen meats, raised, killed and packaged from one farm in Yorkshire. Plus that rude county's partridge, hare and venison, vegetables and fruit.

Wainwright & Daughter
359 Fulham Rd, SW3 (352 0852)
Mon-Sat 8.00-6.00.
Good quality butchers and greengrocers. The fishmonger part stocks live eels.

Whittards
111 Fulham Rd, SW3 (589 4261)
Mon-Fri 8.15am-6.00.
Tea and coffee sellers in atmosphere of an old packing house. Shelves of honeys, fine tinned foods and chocolates.

HOME

Conran
77/79 Fulham Rd, SW3 (589 7416)
Mon-Sat 9.30am-6.00.

The best of the modern classics — furniture to glass; specialist shop to Habitat's supermarket. The style is a mixture of antique, clever copies of the originals (pale geometric rugs based on Eileen Gray designs, Savoy trolleys, American stick furniture) and bright new moderns. Addictive but not cheap.

Ganeesha
6 Park Walk, SW3 (352 8972)
Mon-Sat 11.00am-7.00.
Glories of the Eastern non mass-produced spill on to the pavement, Thai pots, Indian make-up, Chinese drawstring trousers, shadow puppets, textiles, spices and kitchen utensils.

L'Herbier De Provence
341 Fulham Rd, SW10 (352 0012)
Tue-Sat 10.00am-7.00, Mon and Thu 2.30-7.00.
Herbs medicinal (wild pansy, black alder), culinary (five peppers, lemon grass), and teatime (peppermint, almond) in huge sacks. Also thick honeys, sharp sauces, pungent green olive oil, natural sponges, olive oil soap and jams from water melon to sour cherry.

Mary Fox Linton
247 Fulham Rd, SW10 (351 0273)
Mon-Fri 9.15am-5.30, Sat 10.00am-4.00.
Interior designer whose small furniture and fabrics are mainly cool, calm and pastel with soft geometrics. Best for cushions and dhurries.

London Lighting Co
135 Fulham Rd, SW3 (589 4270)
Mon-Sat 9.30am-6.00.
Where the anglepoise lounges in its rigid modernity and other lights hide in boxes and large light bulbs. Switches and accessories.

Mr Light
275 Fulham Rd, SW10 (352 7525)
Mon-Sat 9.30am-6.30.
Innovative light shop — stripes of bright neon, animals for children, kite lights, bright enamel shades and kitsch ceramic lights. Some industrial chic accessories.

Poster Shop
168 Fulham Rd, SW10 (373 7294)
Mon, Tue & Sat 10.00am-6.30, Wed-Fri 10.00am-9.00.
Dedicated to rescuing the poster from its cultural bathos. American jazz posters, Polish circus, exhibition and theatrical events. Framing service.

The Telephone Shop
339 Fulham Rd, SW10 (352 4574)
Mon-Sat 10.00am-6.30.
London's first specialist telephone shop. New York, pay ups, sober black Edwardians, Mickey Mice, and the latest whizz-kids device for the harassed business man.

KING'S ROAD

ANTIQUES

Antiquarius
15 Flood St, SW3 (351 1145)
Mon-Sat 10.00am-6.00.
Covered antiques market selling Art Deco, jewellery, watches, fountain pens, Victoriana, 60s ephemera and period clothes.

CHILDREN

Tiger Tiger
219 King's Rd, SW10 (352 8080)
Mon-Sat 10.00am-6.00.
Old-fashioned toyshop with everything from penny toys to a giant Russian bear. Specialises in doll's houses and puppets and is also a great place to find jokes, six foot long rubber snakes, masks, face paints etc.

CLOTHES

Manolo Blahnik
49/51 Old Church St, SW3 (352 8622)
Mon-Sat 10.30am-6.30.
King of the toe leather. Manolo Blahnik's immaculate shop is a must for all shoe crazies even if only for an envied peep.

Boy
153 King's Rd, SW3 (351 1115)
Mon-Sat 10.00am-6.00.
Almost a curiosity shop but still sneering with punk. Where to go to get the torn and angry clothes.

Edina & Lena
141 Kings Rd, SW3 (352 1085)
Mon-Sat 10.00am-6.00.
Knitwear designers with unflagging imagination. The first people to release the Fair Isle from its bleak Northern stronghold. Soft, laced and traditional rather than chunky and aggressive.

Johnson's
406 King's Rd, SW10 (351 3268)
Mon-Sat 10.30am-6.30.
The Modern Outfitters, famed for their theatrical suits and 50s slick in Gothic surrounds. Downstairs their own boots and shoes for those serious about quiffs.

Kamikaze
27 Sloane Sq, SW3 (730 7050)
Mon-Sat 10.00am-6.30, Wed 10.00am-7.30.
Once Elle, then Tutto now selling the bold, bright clothes by the Italian designer. Tempting but expensive.

Kickers
331 Kings Rd, SW3 (352 7541)
Mon-Sat 10.00am-6.00.
The first of the London shops selling the bright and durable French boots. Always good for tough summer canvas. Also at 15 The Market, Covent Garden, WC2; 183a Beauchamp Place, SW3; 66 South Molton St, W1.

Liberated Lady
408 King's Rd, SW10 (351 3055)
Mon-Sat 10.0am-6.30.
Hula-hoopin' shop full of plastic minis, mean spex, glo-sox and glorious Technicolor wigs. 60s retros love it.

Meeneys
241 King's Rd, SW3 (351 4171)
Mon-Sat 10.00am-6.00.
Where the great American sweat shirt marches onward. Cowboy shirts, Osh Kosh butcher stripe dungarees, padded vests, boots and braces. Best for kids.

Natural Shoe Store
325 King's Rd, SW3 (351 3721)
Mon-Sat 10.15am-6.00.
Shoes for buffeting pavements — hiking and cowboy boots, fine English leather, Chinese slippers and clogs. Also at 21 Neal St, WC2; 21 North End Rd, W14.

Rider
231 King's Rd, SW3 (351 3198)
Mon-Sat 10.15am-6.00.
Excellent shoes, mostly pumps and boots by Walkers and Pancaldi. Also at 8 South Molton St, W1; 201 Sloane St, SW1.

Robot
323 King's Rd, SW3 (352 6499)
Mon-Sat 10.00am-6.00.
Find the rock shoes behind the blue shuttered windows. Creepers and crepers and buckled suede, plus neat coloured shirts, suits in their own fabrics, bow ties and socks.

Twentieth Century Box
357 King's Rd, SW3 (351 0724)
Mon-Sat 11.30am-6.30.
In spite of its location at the wide World's End, Twentieth Century Box abounds with infinite variety without outrageous labels or price tags. Recognise it by the rack of old coats flapping in a

creaking wind and piles of bright deco china in the window. Inside trilbies, cricket trousers, crombies, brogues and blazers, dinner suits, cravats and Gladstone bags. Do not miss the 30s radios, cocktail shakers, canes and strange teapots.

HOME

Designer's Guild
277 King's Rd, SW3 (351 1271)
Mon-Fri 9.30am-5.30, Sat 10.00am-4.00.
Fabric and wallpaper in a welter of pretty matching pastels and flowers. Downstairs for a fine range of dhurries and spotted china.

Habitat
206/222 King's Rd, SW3 (351 1211)
Mon-Sat 9.30am-6.00, Thu 10.00am-5.30.
The largest outpost of the Conran empire, he who made modern design compulsive. Three floors of furnishings, lighting, kitchen equipment, toys, flooring and a leafy restaurant. Also at 156 Tottenham Court Rd, W1; King's Mall Shopping Centre, Hammersmith, W14.

Liberty's Print Shop
340a King's Rd, SW3 (352 6581)
Mon-Sat 9.30am-6.00, Wed 9.30am-6.30.
If you can't make it to the main store in Regent St, unfold the rich rolls of cloth here — the famous Liberty print, varuna wool and cottons.

David Mellor
4 Sloane Sq, SW1 (730 4259)
Mon-Sat 9.30am-5.30.
Specialist kitchen shop with equipment for plain to gourmet cooking. Excellent for English country baskets, craft pottery and glass. Also at 22 James St, WC2.

Osborne & Little
304 King's Rd, SW3 (352 1456)
Mon-Fri 9.30am-5.30, Sat 10.00am-4.00.
Original wallpapers and fabrics. If you're fed up with the same wall, change them here.

Scribblers
170 King's Rd, SW3 (351 1173)
Mon-Sat 10.00am-6.30.
One of the few shops in London with a good graphic eye. Get the birthday card here, American imports, witty wrapping paper, postcards and briefcases.

Yves Rocher
132 King's Rd, SW3 (581 0675)
Mon-Fri 10.00am-6.00, Sat 10.00am-5.30.
Beauty Centre shining in green and white, selling the best of French natural beauty products. Also at 9 Gees Court, W1.

WHERE TO REST YOUR FEET

Habitat Cafe
206 Kings Rd, SW3
Leafy, tiled, quiche and fruit juice cafe that lives up to the Conran good taste.

Blushes
52 Kings Rd, SW3
Crammed chequered tables, food (pinkish beef and passion cake) and wine upstairs, cocktails downstairs. Watch the fashion here, everybody else does.

Parsons
311 Fulham Rd, SW10
Magnolia paint, Empire fans, potted plants, spaghetti, burgers, raw wine and rock.

TRANSPORT

(All details subject to change. Phone 01-222 1234 at anytime, day or night to check details. Some routes shown do not operate every day of the week.)

Tube: Sloane Square, South Kensington
Buses: 11, 14, 19, 22, 31, 39 (Mon-Sat only, except evenings), 45, 49, 137
Night: N97

1. Pan Bookshop
2. Chelsea Design Co
3. Laura Ashley
4. Brother Sun
5. Butler & Wilson
6. Great Expectations
7. Night Owls
8. Piero Di Monzi
9. Tatters
10. Hundred Acre Farm Shop
11. Wainwright & Daughter
12. Whittards
13. Conran
14. Ganeesha
15. L'Herbier de Provence
16. Mary Fox Linton
17. London Lighting Co
18. Mr Light
19. Poster Shop
20. The Telephone Shop
21. Antiquarius
22. Tiger Tiger
23. Manolo Blahnik
24. Boy
25. Edina & Lina
26. Johnson's
27. Kamikaze
28. Kickers
29. Liberated Lady
30. Meeneys
31. Natural Shoe Store
32. Rider
33. Robot
34. Twentieth Century Box
35. Designers Guild
36. Habitat
37. Liberty Prints
38. David Mellor
39. Osborne & Little
40. Scribblers
41. Yves Rocher

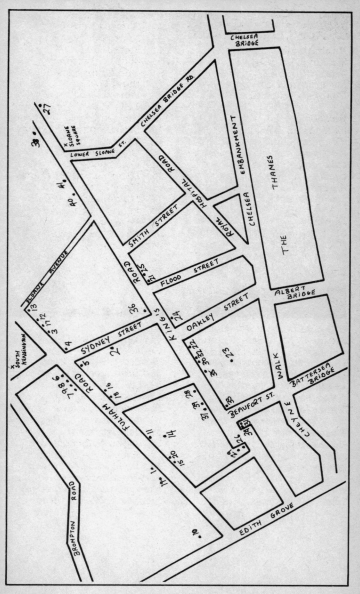

KNIGHTSBRIDGE

At the end of the grand green space of Hyde Park lies the Knightsbridge, land of the flying fur and squealing taxi where the Huskies roam all day. And Harrods, its great flagship zipped by a thousand lights, a dome full of elephants and pins lifting to a receding sky. If you cannot face the effor which must always be the West End, find the designers here in duplicate (Browns, Joseph, Fiorucci). Stalk Sloane Street and Brompton Road for rich letaher (Fendi, Loewe, Charles Jourdan) and Beauchamp Place for tiny windows shining with party taffeta (Lucy's, Panache, Spaghetti, Regamus). Art Decos walk to the edge of Belgravia and find Halkin Arcade, tired feet shake their chequebooks and have pretty lunches in Walton Street.

CENTRES

General Trading Co
144 Sloane St, SW1 (730 0411)
Mon-Sat 9.00am-6.00, Wed
9.00am-7.00.
*Department store for gifts,
especially for garden
furniture, china and toys.
Where the Sloane Rangers
have their wedding lists.*

Harrods
Brompton Rd, SW1 (730 1234)
Mon-Sat 9.00am-6.00, Wed
9.00am-7.00.
*Harrods can inspire anything
from love to anger; most
people keep cool, call it
Horrids but always go back.
Harrods grabs all the
superlatives, it is the largest
store in Europe, it has its own
bank, the last circulating
library in London, was the first
to have an in-store pub and
escalators and the greatest
range of butter in the world. If
you can't bear the smug
grandeur of it all, go to the
piano department (150 kinds),
the pet department that once
had all manner of exotic
beasts but now sticks to the
domestic sort and orders the
rest, the excellent Book
department and the Food
Halls. These marbled
chambers have the best
sellable feast in the city — 450
kinds of cheese, 130 kinds of
bread, 85 different brands of
malt whisky, a great game
table, fruit out of season and in
Christmas 1979 sold 85,000
plum puddings. If just looking,
don't miss the fish display
designed afresh by the buyer
every morning on his return*
*from Billingsgate and the
magnificently tiled Meat Hall
festooned with salami.*

Harvey Nichols
Knightsbridge, SW1 (235 5000)
Mon-Sat 9.30am-6.00.
*Harvey Nichols is
Knightsbridge's other store
but no less for it. Best for
clothes and accessories
especially of the designer sort.*

ANTIQUES

Dragons
25 Walton St, SW1 (589 3795)
Mon-Fri 9.30am-5.30, Sat
10.00am-4.30.
*Antique shop gratefully
without a forbidding window,
instead filled with delicious
old things mainly from
Georgian London. Dragons
also paint children's furniture,
chairs, toyboxes, clocks with
names and decorations, make
Surrey fenders to order and
hand-cast brass replicas of
Queen Anne lamps.*

Jarrolds
24 Brompton Arcade, SW1
(599 2200)
Mon-Fri 9.15am-4.45, Sat
9.15am-12.45.
*Leather of the straighter sort
— wallets, visitors' books.
Services include rethreading
pearls, making fan and medal
cases and painting miniatures.*

BOOKS

Truslove & Hanson
205 Sloane St, SW1 (235 2128)
Mon 9.00am-5.30, Wed
10.00am-7.00, Sat 10.00am-5.00.

Good general bookshop,
especially for fiction.

CHILDREN

La Mecedora
11 Brompton Arcade, SW1
(589 0889)
Mon-Sat 9.30am-6.00.
Ablaze with expensive
children's clothes from Spain,
hand-smocked dresses, snappy
co-ordinates in primary
colours, leather shoes, fine
and laced selection of
christening and communion
dresses.

Mome
27 Harrington Rd, SW7 (589
8306)
Mon-Fri 9.30am-5.30, Sat
9.30am-4.00
Expensive well made clothes
for children who like to fly a
continental label.

CLOTHES

Benetton
23 Brompton Rd, SW1 (589 2123)
Mon-Sat 10.00am-6.30, Wed
10.00am-7.00.
Modern classic Italian knitwear
— best in plain, sharp colours.
Also at 6 South Molton St.

Browns
6c Sloane St, SW1 (235 7973)
Mon-Sat 10.00am-6.00, Wed
10.00am-7.00.
The designer's place. Also at
23/26 South Molton St.

Fiorucci
15 Brompton Rd, SW1 (584
4095)
Mon-Fri 10.00am-6.30, Wed

10.00am-7.30, Sat 10.00am-6.00.
Clothes and accessories in hi-
splash colour, wit and kitsch.
Also at 133 New Bond St.

Joseph
6 Sloane St, SW1 (235 2467)
Mon-Sat 9.30am-6.00, Wed
9.30am-7.00.
Joseph's hi-tech space, hung
with brilliant utility clothes and
knits. Also at 13 South Molton
St.

Kenzo
23 Brompton Arcade, SW1
(584 1857)
Mon-Sat 9.30am-6.00, Wed
9.30am-7.00.
Where the Mikado of mix and
match sells the dazzling cloth.

Monsoon
35 Beauchamp Place, SW1
(589 7737)
Mon-Sat 10.00am-6.00, Wed
10.00am-7.00.
Floating dresses from the East,
rich colours, hand-printed,
silks and cottons. Also at 67
South Molton St, W1; 54
Fulham Rd, SW3; 1 Hampstead
High St, NW3; 23 The Market,
Covent Garden, WC2.

Whistles
14 Beauchamp Place, SW3
(581 4830)
Mon-Sat 10.00am-6.00, Wed
10.00am-7.00.
Zany sportswear, inventive
knits, dashing labels. Also at 1
Thayer St, W1; 20 The Market,
Covent Garden, WC2.

FOOD

Bendicks
195 Sloane St, SW1 (235 4749)

Mon-Fri 9.00am-5.30, Sat
9.00am-3.30.
*Home of the imperial
bittermint, plus hand-made
chocolates and military block
chocolate. Also at 53 Wigmore
St, W1; 20 Royal Exchange,
EC3.*

Bonne Bouche
22 Bute St, SW7 (584 9839)
Mon-Sat 9.00am-6.00
*In South Kensington's tiny
delicious food street, Bonne
Bouche is worth a stop for its
patisserie but more particularly
for the granary baguettes and
black bread. Also at Thayer St,
W1 (plus tea room).*

Justin De Blank's Hygienic Bakery
46 Walton St, SW3 (589 4734)
Mon-Fri 7.30am-6.00, Sat
7.30am-1.00.
*Real bread baked in 100-year
old ovens: crusty white, dark
rye and butter croissants.*

German Food Centre
44 Knightsbridge, SW1 (235
5760)
Mon-Fri 9.00am-5.30, Sat
9.00am-5.00.
*Sauerkraut, sausage, cheese; a
myriad of breads and sweet
wines from the Rhine.*

Partridges
132 Sloane St, SW1 (730 0651)
Mon-Sat 9.00am-8.00, Sun
10.00am-8.00.
*Grand grocer with extremely
useful opening hours. Treat
yourself to ham on the bone,
glace fruits, rich pates and
smoked salmon.*

Scandinavian Shop
170 Brompton Rd, SW1

(589 7804)
Mon-Sat 9.30-5.30.
*Downstairs for pickled herring
in jars, jams, liqueurs and
variegated crispbreads. Up for
bleak-cut glass, the Marimekko
label and thick oiled
Norwegian fishing sweaters.*

HOME

L'Artisan Parfumeur
194/6 Walton St, SW3 (584
9632)
Mon-Sat 10.00am-6.00.
*Catch the scent of seventeen
different fruits, flowers and
woods in burning oils, room
sprays, bath oils, fans of
vetiver, glass caskets of pot
pourri, terracotta pomanders
of heady amber and silk
cushions of crushed sleep
herbs. Decadent but
compulsive.*

Nina Campbell
48 Walton St, SW3 (584 9401)
Mon-Fri 10.00am-6.00, Sat
10.00am-5.00.
*For those heavily into
prettiness and giftiness: Italian
stationery and marbled boxes,
tissue holders, fluted water
carafes, cushions to scatter,
lamps to recline by, charming
china and wallpaper pictures.*

Danish House
16 Sloane St, SW1 (235 9868)
Mon-Sat 9.30am-5.30.
*Everything for the earnest
needlewoman sitting by the
blazing stove. Hundreds of
embroidery designs, canvas
by the metre, traditional
Danish crafts, books and
candles to light a gloomy
stairway.*

71

Deschamps
197 Sloane St, SW1 (235 6957)
Mon-Sat 9.15am-6.00, Wed
9.15am-7.00.
*Flower-sprigged French cotton
and pastel towelling for the
fresh, pretty bathroom, kitchen
and bedroom. Also for thick
rainbow-coloured towels and
nightdresses.*

**Forces Help Society and Lord
Robert's Workshops**
122 Brompton Rd, SW1
(589 3243)
Mon-Fri 9.00am-5.00.
*Household items made by
disabled war veterans,
brushes to tables. Some of the
finest and cheapest English
basketware in London.*

London Bedding Centre
26/27 Sloane St, SW1 (235 7542)
Mon-Fri 9.00am-5.30, Wed
9.00am-7.00, Sat 9.00am-5.00.
*If you have a problem with a
bed whether it be back ache
or awkward space, this place
will solve it. New designs,
wacky ideas, round beds etc.*

Reject Shop
245 Brompton Rd, SW3 (584
7611)
Mon-Sat 9.45am-6.00, Wed
9.45am-7.00.
*The Reject Shop's success is
partly due to that part in
humanity which is irresistibly
attracted to the idea of a
bargain (only perfectionists
notice the flaws). Piles of
china, furniture and kitchen
equipment. Some ends of lines
and seconds. Also at 209
Tottenham Court Rd, W1.*

Walton Street Stationery Co
97 Walton St, SW3 (589 0777)

Mon-Fri 9.00am-6.00, Sat
9.00am-5.00.
*Where the man of property
gets notepaper headed, plus
innovative cards, gift-wrap,
fine writing paper, pens and
inks.*

1. General Trading Co
2. Harrods
3. Harvey Nichols
4. Dragons
5. Jarrolds
6. Truslove & Hanson
7. La Mecedora
8. Mome
9. Benetton
10. Browns
11. Fiorucci
12. Joseph
13. Kenzo
14. Monsoon
15. Whistles
16. Bendicks
17. Justin de Blank's
    Hygienic Bakery
18. Bonne Bouche
19. German Food Centre
20. Partridges
21. Scandinavian Shop
22. L'Artisan Parfumer
23. Nina Campbell
24. Danish House
25. Deschamps
26. Forces Help Society &
    Lord
27. London Bedding Centre
28. Reject Shop
29. Walton Street Stationery
    Co

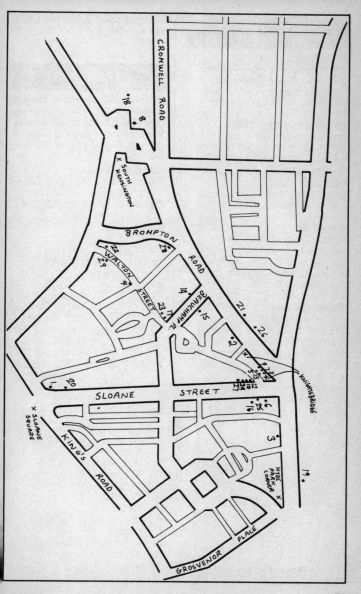

WHERE TO REST YOUR FEET

If you cannot bear the squeeze/queue/large green bag/shrill voice situation at the excellent Harrod's Circles or Health Juice Bar, try these.

General Trading Cafe
General Trading Co 144 Sloane St, SW1
Creamy gateaux, coffee, squidgy spinach quiche, fish mousses, salads with imagination and a balcony for bright weather.

Bendicks
195 Sloane St, SW1
Croque Monsieur, trout, hot chocolate, red plush chairs, mirrors and the old Ladies of the borough.

The Loose Box
7 Cheval Pl, SW1
Where the horsey set after a tiring morning upon the Knightsbridge fields rest a while. Generous portions of cold beef, hot rabbit, seafood vol au vents, chocolate mousse and dynamic wine list. Downstairs for stable decor Waldorf salads, shepherd's pie and sandwiches but the same wine.

TRANSPORT

(All details subject to change. Phone 01-222 1234 at anytime, day or night to check details. Some routes shown do not operate every day of the week.)

KNIGHTSBRIDGE

Tube:	Knightsbridge, Sloane Square
Buses:	9. 14, 22, 30, 52, 52a, 73, 74, 137
Night:	N97

VICTORIA

Tube:	Victoria, Sloane Square
Buses:	2, 2b, 10, 11, 16, 24, 25, 29, 36, 36b, 38, 39, 52, 52a, 55, 70, 76 (Mon-Fri only), 149 (Mon-Fri except evenings), 185, 500 (daily, but not evenings or Sun), 507
Night:	N84, N90, N93, N95, N98 — to Victoria
Or:	137 — to Sloane Square
Or:	77a, 88 — to Pimlico

VICTORIA & PIMLICO

EATON TERRACE

In the middle of Victoria sits the station of that name like a grim anarchic spider where the homeless sit huddled with pidgeons and the travellers depart for Venice, Paris, Istanbul. Victoria Street, blocks of office granite and glass is famous for hiding the soft redbrick of Westminster Cathedral but makes for dull shopping (find the main store at the Army & Navy). Instead turn for specialist shops to Pimlico's Legoland of sour grey brick and butterfly paint door, with the Thames like an oozing serpent and the neo-classic portals of the Tate Gallery, or to the whiter more aristocratic facades of Belgravia, embassies, expensive greengrocers, where the Guard march each day, having changed, to the music of fife and drum.

BOOKS

Belgravia Books
43 Elizabeth St, SW1 (730 5086)
Mon-Fri 10.00am-6.00, Sat
10.00am-1.00.
*Small, informed general
bookshop, best for new fiction
and children's books.*

CHILDREN

Hippo Hall
65 Pimlico Rd, SW1 (730 7710)
Mon-Sat 9.30am-5.00.
*Interior design for concept
nurseries, wallpaper, fabrics,
cushions of anthropomorphic
pattern and bright colour. The
main song is their naif-painted
furniture (desks, nursery
rhyme chairs, cupboards as
doll's houses, beds as double
decker buses) and murals by
commission. Don't miss their
animal alphabet transfers
for boring T-shirts.*

CLOTHES

Cornucopia
12 Tachbrook St, SW1 (828 5752)
Mon-Fri 10.30am-6.00,
Sat 11.00am-6.00.
*Intriguing jungle of second
hand clothes and costume
jewellery.*

Guernseys Galore
49 Moreton St, SW1 (834 6141)
Mon-Sat 9.00am-6.30.
*The ubiquitous sea-jumper in
all sizes and colours, plus
striped Bretons, tough
moleskin trousers, thick socks
for foul weather and wool
hats.*

Mexicana
89 Lower Sloane St, SW1 (730
3871)
Mon-Fri 9.30am-5.30, Sat
10.00am-1.00.
*Where rich little Carmens buy
the fabric of romance. Pin
tucked lace-fretted dresses
and blouses imported from
Mexico in startling black,
white or vivid plain colour.
Often used as wedding
dresses.*

The Sale Shop
2 Barnabus St, SW1 (730 5913)
Mon-Sat 10.00am-5.30, Wed
10.00am-7.00
*International designer clothes
of the dernier cri at wholesale
prices. A sharp eye and rapid
turnover without the manic
cash and grab usually
connected with sales. Mostly
classics and silk shirts,
eccentrics will feel out of place.
Also at 5 Park Walk, SW10.*

FOOD

Justin de Blank
42 Elizabeth St, SW1 (730 0605)
Mon-Fri 9.30am-7.30, Sat
9.30am-2.00.
*One of the first self-conscious
gourmet delicatessens. Find
European vegetables and
salads, jungle fruits, bottled
fruits, French butter, lunch-
time exotica for those gone
beyond the ham sandwich,
deep-frozen gourmet dishes
for cheating suppers, wines,
liqueurs, vinegars, decadent
jams, obscure honeys and
their main delight, French
cheeses. See also J de B's
**Herbs, Plants and Flowers
Shop** at no 42, for growing,*

sprinkling, infusing, seasoning and paying for the style.

Mainly English
14 Buckingham Palace Rd, SW1 (828 3967)
Mon-Fri 10.30am-7.00, Wed 10.30am-5.45.
Specialist shop for noble promotion of English cheese and wines (cynics there are 60 of them). Obscure country cheeses, plus ciders, pickles, jams, home-made pates, hams and herb sausages.

Tachbrook Street Market
Tachbrook St, SW1.
Mon-Fri 9.00am-5.00.
Strong vegetable market with much pavement charm, peppered with seafood stalls, fresh flowers and junk.

HOME

After Dark
64 Pimlico Rd, SW1 (730 9136)
Mon-Fri 10.00am-6.00.
Pimlico Road is awash with the eternal feminine, flower-sprigged prints, broderie anglaise, co-ordinating tissue holders and pretty china of indeterminate function. After Dark, who are no exception, celebrate the bedroom of the seamed rather than seamy sort — handpainted silk sheets, tapestry cushions, nightdresses, lampshades and other sweet dreams.

Casa Pupo
56 Pimlico Rd, SW1 (730 7111)
Mon-Sat 9.30am-6.00.
The first of the Hispanics, Casa Pupo still sell those rugs and cabbage-carved bowls. Those

who stalk the stark, white patio, al fresco scenario will take the plant pots, lamp stands, large china animals pretending to be doorstops and ceramics. A modern print gallery is on the first floor.

Elizabeth David
46 Bourne St, SW1 (730 3123)
Mon-Sat 9.30am-5.30.
England's greatest cookery writer, Elizabeth David stocks the basement with kitchen equipment from France where good food is not just a rare occurence for guests. Huge glittering saucepans, copper pans, le Creuset pans, jelly bags, marble cheese rounds, Sabatier knives...everything a home or restaurant kitchen could want.

Just Gingham
44 Pimlico Rd, SW1 (730 2588)
Mon-Fri 9.30am-6.00, Sat 10.00am-4.00.
Those happy prairie squares in household shapes, lined moses baskets for mix and match babies, hobby horses, smocked sundresses, tiles, jam jar tops, wallpapers and rolls of cloth.

Inca
45 Elizabeth St, SW1 (730 7941)
Mon-Fri 10.00am-6.00, Sat 10.00am-1.00.
Home of Peruvian craftwork from vegetable-dyed geometric rugs and jazz-weave straw baskets to bamboo pipes and alpaca wool jumpers.

Meadow Herbs Shop
47 Moreton St, SW1 (821 0094)

Mon-Thu 9.00am-5.30, Fri
9.00am-5.00.
*English herbs hiding in a
myriad of cushions, oils and
essences extracted without
cruelty to animals, pot pourri
kits. The smell will knock you
over.*

Rain
42 Pimlico Rd, SW1 (730 3318)
Mon-Sat 10.00am-6.00.
*Interior decoration with
Eastern slant, bamboo, leaf-
inspired wallpaper and fabrics
and witty ceramics.*

Upstairs Shop
22 Pimlico Rd, SW1 (730 3318)
Mon-Sat 10.00am-6.00.
*More bedroom furnishings
ablaze with pastels and frills.
For patchwork persons,
Upstairs sell end-of-metre
remnants in most materials
and quilting.*

WHI Tapestry Shop
85 Pimlico Rd, SW1 (730 5366)
Mon-Fri 9.30am-5.00.
*The Tapestry place where the
designs are modern, inspired
by the past, in squares for
carpets, made to order and all
hand-painted, plus wools, plain
canvas, kits and frames.*

WHERE TO REST YOUR FEET

Tate Gallery Cafe
Tate Gallery Millbank, SW1
*Having done the Turner, the
Blakes, the Pre-Raphaelites, the
Pops and the Bricks, grab a cup
of restoritive coffee and
succumb to a wicked slice of
fudge cake. If you had money
enough and time, you would
eat in the excellent Tate
restaurant upon delicacies
Elizabethan and Medieval
culled from the British Museum
and the famous wine list.*

Ebury Wine Bar
139 Ebury St, SW1
*Thick soups, cold meats, a
crusty loaf and a cold glass of
Sauvignon set amongst the
rigid pale facades of Belgravia.*

TRANSPORT

**(All details subject to change.
Phone 01-222 1234 at anytime,
day or night to check details.
Some routes shown do not
operate every day of the
week.)**

Tube:	Victoria, Sloane Square
Buses:	2, 2b, 10, 11, 16, 24, 25, 29, 36, 36b, 38, 39, 52, 52a, 55, 70, 76 (Mon-Fri only), 149 (Mon-Fri except evenings), 185, 500 (daily, but not evenings or Sun), 507
Night:	N84, N90, N93, N95, N98 — to Victoria
Or:	137 — to Sloane Square
Or:	77a, 88 — to Pimlico

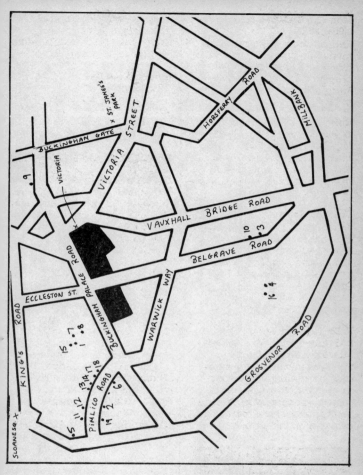

1. Belgravia Books
2. Hippo Hall
3. Cornucopia
4. Guernseys Galore
5. Mexicana
6. The Sale Shop
7. Justin de Blank
8. Justin de Blank's Herbs, Plants and Flowers
9. Mainly English
10. Tachbrook Street Market
11. After Dark
12. Casa Pupo
13. Elizabeth David
14. Just Gingham
15. Inca
16. Meadow Herbs Shop
17. Rain
18. Upstairs Shop
19. WHI Tapestry Shop

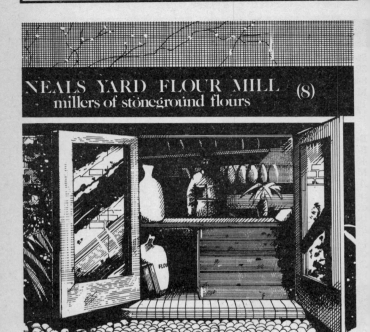

NEALS YARD FLOUR MILL (8)
millers of stoneground flours

NEAL'S YARD

Covent Garden is a space everyone wants of their own but is ever eclipsed by the unwanted crowd. Where once crates of cabbage were flung in the dark, sharp mornings and the writers met the actresses in the crowded coffee houses, there are now gourmet shops and brasseries with light boxes on the wall. The old guard still come here to have their trophies inscribed, their pictures framed, to buy stamps and first editions for their collections and to dine at Rules after a little Verdi at the Opera. But it became the land of publishers and studios where the nouveau avant garde lived. They who took classes at the Pineapple Dance Centre, met at the Photographers' Gallery, read and wrote the magazines, grabbed media cocktails and the quickest bottles of Beaujolais Primeur. That was until the pneumatic drills which had mixed so charmingly with the rehearsal pianos suddenly stopped and the old fruit and vegetable market that had moved six years previously was replaced by a new shopping complex, busy with cafes and street theatre. So Covent Garden began to lure the tourist and sell its England by the pound.

BOOKS

Stanley Gibbons
399 The Strand, WC2 (836 8444)
Mon-Fri 9.30am-5.30, Sat 10.00am-12.30.
Where to find the stamp.

Bernard Stone Turret Bookshop
43 Floral St, WC2 (836 7557)
Mon-Sat 10.00am-7.00.
An addictive bookshop, a perfect blend of ideas, eccentricity and dynamic stock both old and new. Specialising in poetry, the shelves are also rich in children's and detective fiction. Watch out for Sigmund Freud.

CLOTHES

Anello & Davide
30/35 Drury Lane, WC2 (836 1983)
Mon-Fri 10.00am-5.30.
Theatrical hose. Shoes and boots made to fit any historical stage, plus dance shoes, patent pumps and Victorian laced boots.

Bead Warehouse
39 Neal St, WC2 (240 0931)
Mon-Fri 11.30am-6.00, Sat 10.00am-5.30.
Beads of glass, china, stripes, spots, flower, animal, whatever you need you'll find here, including all the wires etc for jewellers.

Cassou
24 Rose St, WC2 (836 6291)
Mon-Sat 9.00am-6.00.
Small accessory and modern jewellery shop. Strings of wooden jewellery, bright scarves and soft leather bags.

Dance Centre
11/14 Floral St, WC2 (836 6544)
Mon-Fri 9.00am-8.00, Sat 9.00am-6.00.
Leotards, tights, leg warmers, towelling tracksuits, dance shoes and all things for the barre and studio floor surrounded by efficient white tile.

Clive Shilton
58 Neal St, WC2 (836 0809)
Mon-Fri 10.00am-7.00, Thu 10.30am-5.30.
Hand-made shoes, boots and bags in 800 different colour combination leathers. Tiny and fiendishly expensive, the price of originality. Also in the Market.

Detail
49 Endell St, WC2 (379 6940)
Mon-Sat 11.00am-7.00.
The place that liberated jewellery from the strong-box. More wit than wealth, more dash than flash, most of the jewellery is made of titanium and plastic, colour and sharp design.

Fifi's Poodle Parlour
44 Wellington St, WC2 (836 4767)
Mon-Sat 10.30am-7.30.
White tile, pink neon ablaze with accessories, kooky spex, mini briefcases, ankle sox, bow ties and leotards.

Flip
125 Long Acre, WC2 (836 9851)

Mon-Sat 10.00am-12 midnight,
Sun 11.00am-6.00.
*The fastest bandwagon in the
West, Flip sell the style
second-hand with a sharp eye
for the street. Kool-aid sweat
shirts, band boy jackets, tweed
flecked overcoats, tuxedos, ski
sweaters, Zippo lighters. The
Wurlitzer blazes and the music
rocks into the night. Chew that
gum. Also at 191 Kings Rd,
SW3 and 96/98 Curtain Rd,
EC2.*

Howie
138 Long Acre, WC2 (240 1541)
Mon-Sat 10.00am-6.30.
*Once one of the great
innovators, Howie has its own
labels plus designers like
Wendy Daworthy. Where to
go to catch Paul Howie's
classic lambswool and hand
knits. Men downstairs.*

Moss Bros
Bedford St, WC2 (240 4567)
Mon-Fri 9.00am (8.30 for
hire)-5.30, Thu 9.00am-7.00, Sat
9.00am-1.00.
*If you haven't got them, hire
the tails here. Formal and
riding clothes and accessories.*

Natural Shoe Store
21 Neal St, WC2 (836 5254)
Mon-Fri 10.00am-6.00, Sat
10.00am-5.30.
*Urban cowboys buy their
mighty Frye Boots here. Other
sensible shoes for hiking,
laced and brogued, Grenson's
fine English leather, Chinese
slippers and espadrilles.*

Paul Smith
44 Floral St, WC2 (379 7133)
Mon-Sat 10.00am-6.00, Thu
10.00am-7.00.

*Excellent shop for men's
clothes. The formula uses
traditional design in modern
colours (10 different each
season). Downstairs soft check
shirts, corduroys, pullovers,
fisher jerseys and Arans.
Upstairs on a quieter classic
front, suits, flannels, sea-island
cotton shirts (striped or plain)
and regimental silk ties. Also
brilliant for hand-fringed
squares, leather braces and
old fountain pens.*

Scottish Merchant
16 New Row (836 2207)
Mon-Sat 10.30am-6.30, Thu
10.30am-7.00, Sat 10.30am-5.00.
*Storm-bravers take the jumper
here. Trad knits from the
fishing outposts, Hebrides and
Channel Islands, Shetland, Fair
Isles, mitts and scarves. Some
designer's wool here, more at
Tomlinson & Tomlinson, 8
Hornton St, W8.*

J Simon
2 Russell St, WC2
(379 7353)
Mon-Sat 10.00am-6.30.
*Corners of the Ivy Leaguers in
this city's version of Brookes
Brothers. Classic clean-cut
American, button down shirts
of snow-white and cool stripe,
navy blazers, shiny loafers.*

Christopher Trill
17 Catherine St, WC2 (836
1319)
Mon-Sat 10.30am-6.00.
*For the sharpest bags. Swing
them with style, gathered
suede, slivers of pewter
leather... the accent
changes. Don't miss
beaten bangles by Pat
Glandville.*

Walkers
116 Long Acre, WC2 (836
9851) 11.00am-6.30.
*Everything under the Walkers
label found here. Brilliant for
suede ankle boots and leather
pumps.*

FOOD

Robert Bruce
19 James St, WC2 (240 0194)
Mon-Fri 8.00am-7.00, Sat
8.00am-6.00.
*Last of the old marketeers by
the corner of the station. Huge
range of fruit and veg, plain to
exotic with daily bargains of
subsiding strawberries,
avocados, melons when in
season. Fresh herbs.*

Coleson
1 Monmouth St, WC2 (836
2066)
Mon-Fri 7.30am-3.00.
*Find the white loaf, all
decadent and crusty at this
delicious baker.*

Cheon Leen Supermarket
4/10 Tower St, WC2 (836 3478)
Mon-Fri 10.00am-7.00, Sat
10.00am-6.00, Sun 12 noon-
5.00.
*Go wok-mad here. Food and
kitchen equipment.*

Drury Tea and Coffee Co
3 New Row, WC1 (836 1960)
Mon-Fri 8.30am-6.00.
*Over 20 blends of coffee,
ground to order. Blended and
unblended teas. Equipment
for both, coffee machines and
teapots and jam for the bread.*

Golden Orient
17 Earlham St, Covent Garden,

WC2 (836 5545)
Mon-Fri 10.00am-6.30, Sat
10.00-5.30.
*Spice and wholefood shop,
especially for Indian cooking.
Dried stuffs, herbs, ghee,
grains, vitamins and honey.*

Hobbs & Co
3 Garrick St, WC2 (240 5653)
Mon-Sat 10.00am-7.00.
*Unashamed gourmandise.
Prepared dishes such as wild
boar with suggested recipes,
balloon jars with rainbow
layers of vegetables, white
truffles, chocolate truffles,
whisky from the barrel.
Excellent for decadent gifts.*

Monmouth Coffee House
27 Monmouth St, WC2
(836 5272)
Mon-Sat 10.00am-6.00.
Bulk beans at a hot price.

**Neal's Yard Whole Food
Warehouse**
2 Neal's Yard (240 1154)
Mon- Sat 10.00am-6.30.
Also Neal's Yard Bakery no 6,
Dairy no 9, Greengrocer no 1
and Flour no 8.
*Holistic produce spills
charmingly on the cobbles,
doves flutter and geraniums sit
in painted window boxes. The
Warehouse is strictly for the
ideological stomach, shelves of
jams with no naughty
preservatives, honey,
chutneys, herbs, dried fruits
and pulses. You won't find any
white bread in the bakery.*

Seven Dials Wine Co
17, Short's Gdns, WC2 (836
9851)
Mon-Fri 11.00am-7.00. Sat
11.00am-6.00.

Owned by the same people as the Monmouth Coffee House, wine is imported in huge tankers and stored under nitrogen in basement vats. Four French wines are then pumped into litre bottles for you (you can bring your own or buy theirs). Tasting allowed. Minimalists love it.

HOME

Astrohome
47/49 Neal St, WC2 (240 0420)
Mon-Sat 10.00am-6.30.
High-tech concepts. This cosmic supermarket sells Harlequin railway china, ice-cream glasses, industrial shelving, camera cases, day-glo plastic bread baskets and astroturf by the metre. Warning: factory style can harm your cheque book.

Badge Shop
18 Earlham St, WC2 (836 9327)
Tue-Fri 11.00am-7.00, Sat 12 noon-6.00.
Badges by the score, including rare and early examples and a badge-making machine for one-offs.

Bland & Sons
21/22 New Row, WC2 (836 9122)
Mon-Fri 9.30am-4.30, Sat 9.00am-11.45.
Gunmakers since 1840. All shooters need a licence.

Catz
25 Bedfordbury, WC2 (836 6513)
Mon-Sat 11.00am-6.00.
For feline freakettes: the cushions, the notepaper, the mugs, the badges, the books, all smiling furrily and making life so sweet. No dogs allowed.

Copper Shop
48 Neal St, WC2 (836 2984)
Mon-Sat 10.00am-6.00.
New versions of the old metal. A shiny array of large kettles, saucepans, warming pans, pots for plants and rustic kitchens. Battered copper retinned and repaired.

Glasshouse
65 Long Acre, WC2 (836 9857)
Mon-Fri 10.00am-6.00, Thu 10.00am-8.00, Sat 11.00am-4.00.
Showcase and workshop of young glassblowers. Watch them here. The Glasshouse also run courses.

Knutz
1 Russell St, WC2 (836 3114)
Mon-Sat 11.00am-8.00.
Anarchic toyshop for Grown-Ups with a sense of humour and love of kitsch.

Inside Out Shop
1 Neal St, WC2 (240 0331)
Mon-Sat 10.00am-12 midnight.
The Inside Out Shop is the Flagship of the Covent Garden Store which also encompasses **The Market Gift Shop,** 26 The Market; **The Grocery Shop,** and **The Pen To Paper Shop** 55 Long Acre. Where a pen is bought because it makes a witty present and hon because it has a pretty label

David Mellor
26 St James St, WC2 (379 6947)
Mon-Sat 10.00am-8.00.
The Renaissance of the Kitchen battles onward against the steak and kidney

pragmatism of the British. David Mellor, Sheffield's master cutler, supplies thoroughly modern knives and forks, a fearsome batterie de cuisine and shelves of fine greenish glass. Those lost amongst the land of Chinese wok and Swedish smoking box will find England well represented in traditional country log and storage baskets and the work of 12 kitchen potters. Take the intelligent, illustrated catalogue home.

Naturally British
13, New Row, WC2 (240 0551)
Mon-Sat 10.30am-7.30.
Awash with the land's culture-past. Upon and about Victorian and Irish cottage furniture unearth pot pourris from Surrey gardens, Dorset chestnut roasters, Cumbrian hand-blown glass, Welsh eel baskets and miners' shirts.

Neal St Shop
23 & 29 Neal St, WC2 (240 0136)
Mon-Sat 10.00am-5.00, Wed 10.00am-7.00.
Specialises in Chinese goods from brilliant rose tin bowls, to old porcelain rice bowls. Plus basket-ware, kite, puppets and jewellery. Great for presents.

Penhaligons
41 Wellington St, WC2 (836 2150)
Mon-Fri 10.00am-6.00, Sat 10.00am-5.00.
William Henry Penhaligon was the Court Barber at the close of Victoria's reign. Penhaligon still use the recipes for perfumes, toilet waters and pomades from his original notebook and make everything in the original way, by hand. Wooden floor and glass-fronted cabinets of Victorian silver-topped bottles, the shop exudes an excellence that is hard to ignore. Try Victorian Posy created especially for the erstwhile Garden Exhibition at the V&A.

Russell & Chapple
23 Monmouth St, WC2 (836 7521)
Mon-Fri 8.30am-5.00.
Extremely practical shop selling artists' and stage canvas, hessians, tarpaulins, twine for parcels and jute for macrame.

Theatre Zoo
28 New Row, WC2 (836 3150)
Mon-Sat 9.00am-5.00.
The mask shop. Where to hire animal masks especially, and costumes, moustaches, make-up and hats for the odd occasion.

Paul Wu
64 Long Acre, WC2 (836 8566)
Mon-Fri 11.00am-6.30, Sat 11.00am-5.30.
Up-market Orientals. Scribblers grasp their pens and inks, cooks their cups for a fragrant jasmine tea and woks for a beautiful fry, and all dilettantes silk flowers and bright mandarin jackets, oiled paper umbrellas for rain, fluttering fans for shine.

SPORTS

The Kite Store
69 Neal St, WC2 (836 1666)

Mon-Sat 10.00am-6.00.
Where to go fly your kite. Kits, frisbees, insect kites from China, elaborate painted kites from Japan, geometric and anthropomorphic.

Covent Garden Cycles
41 Shorts Gdns, WC2 (836 1752)
Mon-Fri 10.00am-7.00, Wed 10.00am-2.30, Sat 10.00am-6.00.
Specialists in commuting and touring bikes. They also sell second-hand or part-exchange, accessories and run a repair service. Always busy.

THE MARKET

The Market opened in the summer of 1980 to roars of disapproval from the angry nostalgics. It was artificial, twee, obvious, expensive, just too much good taste altogether. What they really resented however was that the haven had become a hype and the secret garden had been opened to the public. They had tarmacked the playground and made it safe for the tourists. Still the old arches remain and despite the unashamed consumerism at least it is not another office block, another soulless chain-store shopping precinct and on a good day you can sit and watch jugglers, string quartets and Punch and Judy and never be bored.
One of the conditions of renting space in The Market was that the shops had had commercial and aesthetic success elsewhere. As a result the businesses tend to

be smaller versions of their main branch(es). The craft stalls in the apple market sell ceramics, wood, lace, handknits, fruit, antique clothes etc, and are different every day. The Market opening hours are from 10.00am-8.00, Mon-Sat (stated where different),

BOOKS

Hammicks
1 The Market, WC2 (379 6465)
Good general bookstore, especially for children's books.

Penguin Bookshop
10 The Market, WC2 (379 7650)
Where the famous orange spines roost in shelves of tasty grey and black. Puffins and Pelicans downstairs, new titles upstairs.

CHILDREN

The Dolls House
29 The Market, WC2 (379 7243)
For tiny habitats. Over 500 hand-made items including brushes, rocking horses and antique reproduction furniture. Commissions taken for replicas of your own house.

Pollocks Toy Theatres
44 The Market, WC2 (379 7866)
Mon-Sat 10.00am-7.00.
Upstairs in the land of never-nursery find theatrical prints, Edwardian games, antique dolls, marbles and the cut-out theatres.

Eric Snook
32 The Market, WC2 (379 7681)
Toy-crammed emporium from penny toys for a children's pocket to reproduction German tin toys and Dutch peg dolls for a collector's zeal.

CLOTHES

S Fisher
12 + 18 The Market (836 2576)
For fine traditional cashmere, Fair Isle, Argyle in the right colours. Also menswear and rainwear.

Whistles
20 The Market, WC2 (379 7401)
Though unlike the bank statement, Whistles rarely fails of dazzling ideas. One of the best places to find designer knitwear (Roccoco, Artwork) plus Ally Capellino, Maxfield Parrish leather and Paul Smith's suits for women.

FOOD

W Fenn
6 The Market (379 6427)
Mon- Sat 7.00am-7.00.
Ostensibly an excellent butchers, specialising in poultry and game, Fenn's diversify into a delicatessen, bakers and greengrocer with extremely useful opening hours.

Thornton's
2 The Market, WC2 (836 2173)
The toffee shop. Four varieties of special, brazil, treacle and fruit and nut, plus hand-made chocolates.

HOME

Casa Fina
9 The Market, WC2 (836 0289)
White ceramics, rugs, terracotta pots and wide selection of garden furniture, mainly from Spain, Portugal, Mexico and Italy. Good for white wrought iron on wine and sun-drenched days.

The Candles Shop
30 The Market, WC2 (836 9815)
Mon-Sat 10.00-8.00, Sun 11.00-5.30.
Candles of infinite variety, household white, coloured table, novelty and pure beeswax.

Covent Garden Kitchen Supplies
3 The Market, WC2 (836 9137)
Elizabeth David's shiny and efficient kitchen range. Le Creuset pots, Sabatier knives, marble cheese rounds, jelly bags, icing equipment, French waiters' aprons and everything else devourers of Larousse need and want.

Strangeways
19 The Market, WC2 (379 7675)
Strangeways was the first place to have those cups on legs. The innovation goes on with briefcases, ceramics, witty stationery, bow ties but best for modern clocks and teapots.

BLOOMSBURY

Bloomsbury is famous for blue stockings. Most of the writers have moved out and become journalists but the bookshops are still there under the giant shadow of the British Museum. The streets of literary wandering are Museum St, Charing Cross Rd and Cecil Court.

BOOKS

Dillons
1 Malet St, WC1 (636 1577)
Mon, Thu and Fri 9.00am-5.30,
Tue 10.00am-5.30, Wed
9.00am-7.00, Sat 9.30am-1.00.
As London University's bookshop, Dillons is best for academic tomes. Well-ordered for general topics with a second-hand and bargain department next door.

Foyles
119 Charing Cross Rd, WC1
(836 4207)
Mon-Sat 9.00am-6.00, Thu
9.00am-7.00.
The largest bookshop bruiser in London. If you are tenacious you will be able to find nearly everything here, including books in foreign languages and sheet music.

CHILDREN

Davenports
51 Great Russell St, WC2
(405 8524)
Mon-Fri 9.00am-5.00.

The great magic shop also for adults with a sense of humour and professional magicians. Tricks, itching powder, masks, gruesome spiders and snakes, fireworks. Know it by the metal sign of the rabbit out of a hat.

CLOTHES

James Smith
53 New Oxford St, WC1 (836
4731)
Mon-Fri 9.00am-5.30.
The best shop facade in London. Smith's is the champion of umbrellas, especially the black rolled variety to defy the filthy English rain. Walking and shooting sticks.

Westaway & Westaway
65 Great Russell St, WC1 (405
4479)
Mon-Fri 9.00am-5.30, Sat
9.00am-1.00.
Frenetic Shetlands at a fair price. Other Scottish weaves include kilts, tartan scarves, blankets etc.

FOOD

Continental Stores
54 Tavistock St, WC1 (837
6616)
Mon-Fri 9.00am-6.00, Sat
9.30am-5.30.
As the name suggests, produce of many lands. Salamis, dried herbs, spices, ham on the bone, cheeses and coffees.

Samuel Gordon
76 Marchmont St, WC1 (387 227

Tue-Sat 8.00am-5.30, Thu
8.00am-5.00, Fri 8.00am-6.00,
Sat 8.00am-4.00.
*Good fishmonger. Fresh fish
on the slab, live eels, crabs,
smoked and shell fish.*

HOME

Practical Styling
behind Centrepoint, 13/16 St
Giles High St, W1 (240 3711)
Mon-Tue 10.00am-6.30, Wed-
Fri 10.00am-7.30, Sat
10.00am-6.00.
*Where the industrial chic go
to buy their metal-hardware.
Primary filing cabinets, the
most kitsch floral lino, canteen
cutlery and cartoon dustbins.
Great working bikes in black
and chrome.*

WHERE TO REST
YOUR FEET

*Covent Garden is positively
rife with wine bars,
brasseries, restaurants and
public houses. Here are two
flagships.*

Tuttons
11 Russell St, WC2
*Upstairs the quieter wine bar
and brasserie, downstairs the
restaurant. Floorboards, rock,
menu leaps from kippers to
frog's legs and so do the
prices. Where the pretty
people throw their magazine
smiles and vow they're so
bored with the place but
always come for just one more
Perrier.*

Lamb and Flag
33 Rose St, WC2
Next to the Alley where

*Dryden was mugged, this tiny
old public house spills its
crowd onto a cobbled
courtyard and sells a sharp and
ancient English cheese.*

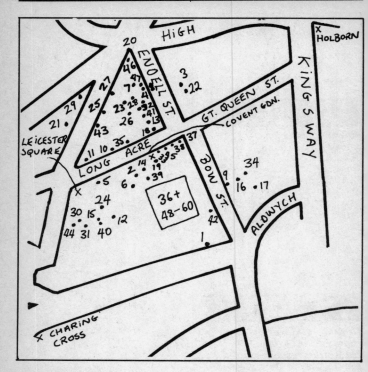

COVENT GARDEN

1. Stanley Gibbons
2. Bernard Stone Turret Bookshop
3. Anello and Davide
4. Bead Warehouse
5. Cassou
6. Dance Centre
7. Clive Shilton
8. Detail
9. Fifi's Poodle Parlour
10. Flip
11. Howie
12. Moss Bros
13. Natural Shoe Store
14. Paul Smith
15. Scottish Merchant
16. J Simon
17. Christopher Trill
18. Walkers
19. Robert Bruce
20. Coleson
21. Cheon Leen Supermarket
22. Drury Tea and Coffee Co
23. Golden Orient
24. Hobbs & Co
25. Monmouth Coffee House
26. Neal's yard Wholefood Warehouse
27. Seven Dials Wine Co
28. Astrohome
29. Badge Shop
30. Bland & Sons
31. Catz
32. Copper Shop
33. Glasshouse
34. Knutz
35. Inside Out Shop

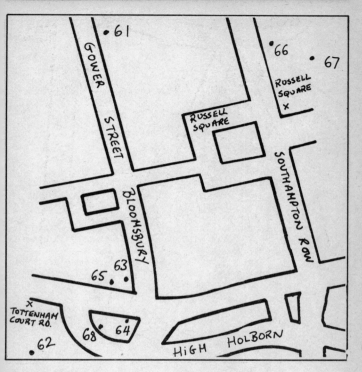

36. Market Gift Shop
37. The Grocery Shop
38. The Pento Paper Shop
39. David Mellor
40. Naturally British
41. Neal St Shop
42. Penhaligons
43. Russell & Chapple
44. Theatre Zoo
45. Paul Wu
46. The Kite Store
47. Covent Garden Cycle Store
48. Hammicks
49. Penguin Bookshop
50. The Dolls House
51. Pollocks Toy Theatres
52. Eric Snook
53. S Fisher

54. Whistles
55. W Penn
56. Thorntons
57. Casa Fina
58. The Candles Shop
59. Covent Garden Kitchen Supplies
60. Strangeways

BLOOMSBURY
61. Dillons
62. Foyles
63. Davenports
64. James Smith
65. Westaway & Westaway
66. Continental Stores
67. Samuel Gordon
68. Practical Styling

COVENT GARDEN & BLOOMSBURY

TRANSPORT

(All details subject to change.
Phone 01-222 1234 at anytime,
day or night to check details.
Some routes shown do not
operate every day of the
week.)

COVENT GARDEN
Tube: Covent Garden
(closed Sun), Leicester
Sq, Charing Cross,
Holborn
Buses: 1, 6, 9, 11, 13 (Mon-Fri
only) 15, 23, 77 (Mon-
Sat only), 77a, 170
(Mon-Fri only, but not
evenings), 172 (Mon-
Sat only), 176 (Mon-Fri
only).
Night: N68, N83, N85, N86,
N87, N88, N91, N92,
N93, N94, N97 — to
Strand
Or: 5, 68, 77a, 170 (Mon-Fri
only, but not
evenings), 172 (Mon-
Sat only), 188, 239
(Mon-Fri only, but not
evenings), 501 (Mon-
Fri only, but not
evenings)
Night: N92 — to Kingsway
Or: 1 (Mon-Fri only, also
Sat shopping hours),
24, 29, 176 (Mon-Fri
only)
Night: N90 — to Charing
Cross Road
Or: 14, 19, 22, 38, 55
Night: N84, N95, N98 — to
Cambridge Circus

BLOOMSBURY
Tube: Russell Sq, Goodge St,
Tottenham Court Rd,
Holborn
Buses: 7 (Mon-Fri only), 8, 14,
19, 22, 24, 25, 29, 38,
55, 68, 73, 77a, 134,
176, 188, 239 (Mon-Fri
only, but not evenings)
Night: N84, N89, N95, N98

HOLBORN & THE CITY

SMITHFIELD MARKET

The City is monuments, pin stripes, twisted streets, dark buildings, financial concrete. Some bowler hats and furled brollies still flow up King William Street before the stroke of nine. But for all its rich historic labelling - - Fleet Street, St Pauls, Cheapside, Threadneedle Street, Pudding Lane, the Old Bailey, the area is poor in shops. It remains a place of work. Best taken in a midnight walk for the architecture and old churches. Leather Lane is the raucous street market, Hatton Garden where the glitterati hit the rocks. The following are worth the trip (but avoid the weekend when everything shuts down and the wind takes over).

BOOKS

Central Books
37 Grays Inn Rd, WC1 (242 6166)
Mon-Fri 9.30am-5.30, Sat 10.00am-12 noon.
Where the hacks catch the facts. Good general bookshop with a slant towards politics. Don't miss their second-hand department for obscure tracts, Russian novels and travel books.

HMSO
49 High Holborn, WC1 (928 6977)
Mon-Fri 8.30am-5.00.
Sober, solid vessel of Governmental prose. Get your Hansard and Ordnance Surveys here. The staff know all the rules.

Skoob Books
15 Sicilian Ave,
Southampton Row, WC1 (404 3063)
Mon-Sat 10.30am-6.30.
Run by the former staff of Pooles in Charing Cross Rd, this shop is a browsers place for antequarian and second-hand books, mainly academic and literary.

CLOTHES

Blax
8 Sicilian Ave, WC2 (404 0125)
Mon-Fri 10.30am-6.30.
Aptly sited amongst the pigeon-soaring archaic arches, Blax sell original clothes from 1910 to late 50s, concentrating on the men. Suits (Edwardian to gangster double breasted),

hats (trilbies, homburgs and felts), plain and coloured shirts, ties (plus their clips and pins), shoes (brogues, Oxfords), jewellery and scarves.

EH Rann
21 Sicilian Ave, WC1 (405 4759)
Mon-Fri 9.00am-5.30.
A thousand educational and regimental stripey ties to gladden the institutional heart. Rann's main speciality is the hand-working of heraldic shields.

FOOD

East West Foods
Community Health Foundation, 196 Old St, E1 (250 1708)
Mon-Fri 10.30am-7.00, Sat 10.30am-5.30.
This Foundation encompasses the holistic rainbow from health bookshop to Earth Mother playgroup. The food store specialises in macrobiotic foods and Japanese imports, including tofu, tempeh and seitan. Aside from soya there are goat dairy products, fruit juices, organic grains and vegetable, rye breads, the ideological bite (tofu parcels, bean pasties) and natural sweets (no sugar) and cosmetics.

Leadenhall Market
Leadenhall St, EC2.
Mon-Fri 7.00am-4.00.
Covered Victorian market for wholesale and retail fish (Ashdown) game, charcuterie and meat (Ashby). Celebrated

by the City worker as an oasis in the concrete desert. Also for cheese, eggs, fruit and veg, pet food and gardening equipment.

Rilla & Cox
8 West Smithfield, EC1 (236 7545)
Mon-Fri 9.00am-6.30, Sat 10.00am-1.00.
Flying in the face of so much red meat, Rilla & Cox are a shiny white shop specialising in cheeses, selling over 200 kinds from a myriad French goat cheese to Shropshire Blue. Also find real French bread and croissants, frozen delights (mussels, scallops, stuffed snails) pickles, preserves coffee beans ground to order, Jacksons teas, terrines, English pies and Ackermans mouth-wicked chocolates. Rilla & Cox also will make up luncheon boxes and hampers for picnics and parties. Also at 5 Theberton St, N1; Ackermans at 9 Goldhurst Terrace, NW6.

Smithfield
Farrington Rd, EC1.
Mon-Fri 5.00am-12 noon.
The city's meat market, swinging with giant carcases. Now that Covent Garden (veg) and Billingsgate (fish) have moved out, get the architecture quick. There are butchers surrounding the market who will not scorn the non-trader but it's still not the place to buy an idle chop or small steak.

Dennis Groves
9 Sicilian Ave, WC2 (405 5603)
Mon-Sat 10.00am-6.00.
Adjustable living, roll-up mattresses, fold up frames, beds that turn into sofas (The Put Down), the platform bed (The Dog)...ideal for those without any space or low-boredom thresholds. Dennis Groves is the city's specialist on scaffold furniture (trestles, platforms, four poster beds); for full range and commissions go to One Off 31 Shorts Gardens, WC2.

The Workshop
83 Lambs Conduit St, WC1 (242 5335)
Mon-Fri 10.30am-5.30, Sat 11.00am-12.30.
Mel Calman's cartoon shop. Stock includes Larry, Honeysett, Posy Simmonds, Calman's own, Paula Youens, Sara Midda, Scarfe and that's not quite all folks. Keep an eye for exhibitions and postcards.

Hubbards
199 Grays Inn Rd, WC1 (837 4366)
Mon-Fri 9.00am-5.00.
Real high-techs discover then paint it themselves. Hubbards sell office furniture in all its Caulfield bleakness: filing cabinets, swivel typists' chairs, directors' desks.

London Architectural Salvage and Supply Co
Mark St, EC2 (739 0376)
Mon-Fri 9.30am-5.30, Sat 10.00am-12.30.
Huge cold church stacked to

the rafters with furniture and fitting from old houses. Great hunting ground for restorers. Stock includes vast claw-footed baths, banisters, wooden flooring, stained glass doors, desks, shutters, school radiators, church pews, and tiled fireplaces.

The Russian Shop
278 High Holborn, WC1 (405 3538)
Mon-Fri 9.15am-5.30, Sat 9.15am-1.00.
Where the balalaika holds sway. Mainly from the USSR, the gifts include the famous shiny nesting dolls, and other wooden toys, stone carvings from the Urals, Bulgarian pokerwork boxes, Ukraine porcelain and all that Zhivago jazz.

SPORTS

Alpine Sports
10/12 High Holborn, WC1 (404 5681)
Mon-Sat 10.00am-6.00, Thu 10.00am-7.00.
Everything for the cross-country skier and mountaineer, ski boots, apres skis, sharp clothes. In summer tennis, watersports (surfboards, wetsuits, windsurfing). Plus rollerskates and BMX bikes. Also at 114 Brompton Rd, SW1 and 215 Kensington High St, W8.

Pindisports
13/18 High Holborn, WC1 (404 0125)
Mon-Sat 9.00am-5.30, Thu 9.00am-7.00.
Wide ranging sports shop but

specialising in climbing, camping and ski wear and equipment. Also at **West One Centre** Oxford St, W1.

Condor Cycles
90 Grays Inn Rd, WC1 (837 7641)
Mon-Fri 9.30am-6.00, closed 2.30-3.30 for lunch, Sat 9.30am-3.00.
Specialist cycle shop. Professional pedal-pushers take their racers, custom-built and DIY bikes here. Also excellent for spare parts, accessories and some very chic wind-resistant cycle clothes.

WHERE TO REST YOUR FEET

El Vino's
47 Fleet St, EC4
Powerhouse of the hacks whose press freedom doesn't extend to entering without a tie or letting the woman order the drinks/sit at the bar. Keep your ears open and sip a schooner of sherry or glass of champagne.

Mother Bunch's
Old Seacoal Lane, EC4
Underneath the grimy arches of Ludgate Circus a verdict's throw from the Old Bailey, this wine house has tough wooden tables, sawdust upon the floor, cold game pâté, prawns, Stilton, smoked fish and cold refreshing white wine and clarets.

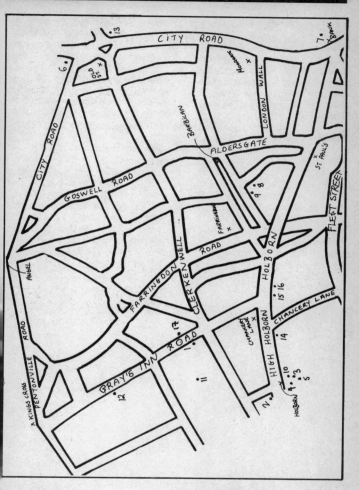

1. Central Books
2. HMSO
3. Skoob Books
4. Blax
5. EH Rann
6. East West Foods
7. Leadenhall Market
8. Rilla & Cox
9. Smithfield
10. Dennis Groves
11. The Workshop
12. Hubbards
13. London Architectural Salvage and Supply Co
14. The Russian Shop
15. Alpine Sports
16. Pindisports
17. Condor Cycles

TRANSPORT

(All details subject to change.
Phone 01-222 1234 at anytime,
day or night to check details.
Some routes shown do not
operate every day of the
week.)

Tube: Holborn, Farringdon,
Moorgate, St Paul's,
Mansion House
Buses: 5, 8, 19, 22, 25, 38, 55,
68, 77a, 170 (Mon-Fri,
but not evenings), 172,
188, 239 (Mon-Fri, but
not evenings), 501
(Mon-Fri only, but not
evenings)
Night: N84, N89, N98 — to
Holborn

Or: 5, 18 (Mon-Sat only,
but not evenings), 19,
38, 45, 46 (Mon-Fri, but
not evenings), also Sat
morning, 55, 63, 168a
(Mon-Fri only), 221
(Mon-Fri only, except
evenings), 243 (Mon-
Sat only, but not Sat
evenings), 259 (Mon-
Sat only) — to
Clerkenwell
Or: 8, 9, 11, 15, 21 (Mon-
Sat only), 22, 25, 43
(Mon-Sat only), 76
(Mon-Sat only), 133,
501 (Mon-Fri, except
evenings), 502 (Mon-
Fri, except evenings)
Night: N89, N91, N94, N95,
N97, N98 — to Bank

EAST OF THE CITY

BRICK LANE MARKET

The East End is a post-industrial animal sprawling greyly about the old docklands, scarred by lorry-screaming arterial roads and tower blocks. Some of the river warehouses have been enlivened with brightly coloured paint and geraniums and used for studio space but an English Soho it is not. Only the bulk wine-houses that are at the edge appear as richer aliens. The East End is full of working people, rag trade and markets. You would not go here to shop but to explore an older more savage London that does not dress itself up for visitors. Some of the architecture is extraordinary (do not miss Spitalfields).

EAST OF THE CITY

FOOD

Rogg
137 Cannon St Rd, E1 (488 3386)
Mon-Fri 9.30am-6.00, Sun 7.00am-4.00.
Great Jewish deli bright with labels in a depressed derelict street, biscuit tins on the wooden shelf, barrels of fresh pickled cucumbers on the stone floor; probably the cheapest smoked salmon in the city in different grades and prices. Take their chopped liver, gefilte fish, rye breads, pickled herrings, salt beef and kippers.

WINE

The East End has several wholesale wine depots where you can taste before you buy but have to take it away by the caseload (except for Balls Bros). They stock a wide range of European wines at cut prices. The crowds arrive on Sundays after the markets, so unless you are crazy about scrabbling for bottles, go during the week.

Balls Bros
Cash and Carry, 313 Cambridge Heath Rd, E2 (739 6466)
Mon-Fri 10.00am-6.00, Sat 10.00am-2.00.

Great Wapping Wine Co
St Helen's Wharf, 60 Wapping High St, E1 (488 3988)
Mon-Sat 11.00am-5.00.

The Noble Grape
26 The Highway, E1 (488 4788)
Mon-Sat 10.00am-6.00, Sun 11.00am-5.00.

CLOTHES

Flip
96/98 Curtain Rd, EC2 (729 4341)
Mon-Sat 10.00am-6.30, Sun 10.00am-3.00.
The grand American used-clothes depot. This old warehouse is piled with the baseball jacket side of Flip's success, more utility than street fashion but less expensive than the other two branches at 191 King's Rd, SW3 and 116 Long Acre, WC2.

HOME

Brick Lane Market
Brick Lane, E1.
Sun morning.
*Over-publicised street market specialising in cheap and shiny clothes, fruit and veg, second hand records, junk in the real sense of the word, huge rolls of crushed marmalade carpets, piles of new saucepans, tinned food being flogged in loud voices, tropical fish, animals and the best stall of kitsch plastic flowers you have ever seen. The tourist and tripper will not find true Cockney London at the famous **Petticoat Lane Market** either, but will find clothes of the nasty and anoraky kind. The best market in the East End is the **Columbia Road Market** in Bethnal Green Rd (also on Sun*

morning) for cut flowers, bedding plants, herbs and compost.

WHERE TO REST YOUR FEET

Blooms
90 Whitechapel High St, E1
Before or after Hawksmoor's brilliant Spitalfield's church and the new art and architecture at the Whitechapel Gallery, take away a thick hot salt beef on rye or stay for best kosher in this famous Jewish restaurant (book for Sundays).

TRANSPORT

All details subject to change. Phone 01-222 1234 at anytime, day or night to check details. Some routes shown do not operate every day of the week.)

Tube: Aldgate, Aldgate East, Liverpool St, Tower Hill

Buses: 5, 10, 15, 22a, 23, 25, 40, 42, 44 (Sun am only), 78, 95 (Sun am only), 253

Night: N84, N95, N98 — to Aldgate

Or: 5, 6, 8, 8a (Mon-Fri only, except evenings), 9, 11, 22, 22a, 35, 47, 48, 55, 67, 78, 149, 243a (Sun only), 279a (Sun only), 502 (Mon-Fri only, except evenings)

Night: N83, N84, N91, N94, N97 — to Liverpool Street

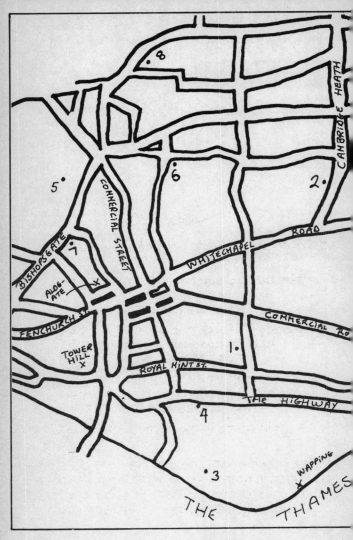

1. Rogg
2. Balls Bros
3. Great Wapping Wine Co
4. The Noble Grape
5. Flip
6. Brick Lane Market
7. Petticoat Lane Market
8. Columbia Road Market

The Body Shop– the natural way to a beautiful body

THE BODY SHOP

"The nicest and most original shop to open"
–WOMAN'S WAY

"The Body Shop Cosmetics are a really sensible range"
–SUNDAY OBSERVER

"The Body shop, where some of the nicest in natural cosmetics originate"
–HERE'S HEALTH

"Since the first Body Shop has been opened the success has been phenomenal"
–SUNDAY TIMES

"A great place to visit"*–SHE MAGAZINE*

Natural based lotions, creams, oils and shampoos packaged in no-nonsense, refillable containers– that's the secret of the Body Shop's incredible success since it first opened five years ago

Body Shops in London
8 Blenheim Crescent, London W1 ● 22/23 Cheapside EC2
65 Kings Road, Chelsea ● 62 Gayton Road, Hampstead
Unit 13 The Market, Covent Garden ● 1A Whitehart Lane, Barnes

DennisGroves FutonFactory

6 layer Futon	topcovers	Standby	Kit
50	15	29.95	38.85
68.50		49.95	
72	20		50.76
85	22		63.40
choice of cover/piping		4 layer	6 layers cotton

The new Putdown; the fully adjustable, all-in-one convertible bed base.

Our futon mattresses and cushions are 6″ thick, made from 6 layers of unbleached pure cotton fibre and contained in a pure cotton cover of natural unbleached calico or a wide choice of coloured cotton drill and tickings. All are available standard or two- tone.

They are manufactured in our workshops to a high seam standard and piped; wide choice available.

All mattresses are tabbed and tufted in traditional British mattress method to keep cotton fill in position; and spaced to provide good folding into sofa shape.

Topcovers

Extra zip-on covers also available.

Kit

In our futon kit, all components are available for self-assembly cushions and mattresses.

It consists of sewn/zipped covers, pre-cut cotton layers, tabs and tufts, and a "rent-a-mattress-needle" (£6 on hire; £5 refund on return).

Loose cotton also available.

The Standby

The 4-layer range, available in calico.

Cotton

Cotton is a natural organic material traditionally used for mattresses in the Far East and Europe.

It is currently regaining wide acceptance because it offers an alternative to foam. Handmade in layers, cotton may be folded or rolled easily into shapes suitable for seating and lends itself particularly well to our Sleepseat, Putdown, and Snake. Or use it straight onto the floor.

Sleepseat

The bedbase consists of two pallets of Portuguese pine, sawn and nailed,

pure cotton fill futons

Dennis Groves 01-405 5603

The new Snake; laid-back and adjustable

using standard pallet manufacturing techniques. They are designed to bed-size specifications and stack and interlock.

With the addition of the slat-back and two webbing straps one of the pallets converts into a sofa and the futon folds into it.

We also offer a smooth, planed version of the same design, which is made to a higher standard.

The range is available in single, double, and kingsize, to take a 6′6″ futon mattress.

Putdown

A new design, it is a logical extension of the original pallet concept; the all-in-one, fully adjustable convertible/bedbase.

Folded it is extremely compact opened it folds from a sofa to recliner to bed.

Available to single, double, and kingsize to take a 6′6″ futon mattress.

Snake

A new design, it folds from bed to recliner and is available in single, double and kingsize to take a 6′ futon mattress.

Both these new designs are produced to a high standard and left a natural planed finish.

Stainbar

New Berger XTP woodstain and water-based matt paint is available in any colour, mixed in our showroom and colour matched.

To order

Phone Jo on 01-405 5603 or visit our Holborn showroom.

Delivery

London area, our van £7 per address, 10-6.

Dennis Groves
9 Sicilian Avenue
Southampton Row, WC1
01-405 5603
Mon-Sat 10-6

London's largest collectio
of antique furniture
under one roof.

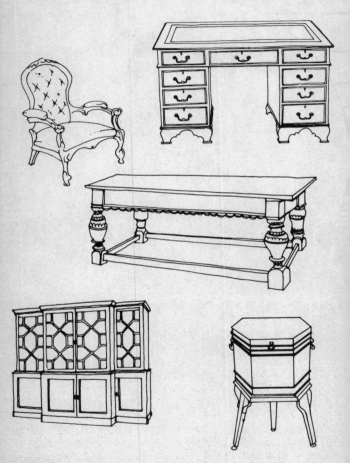

The Furniture Cave

ISLINGTON

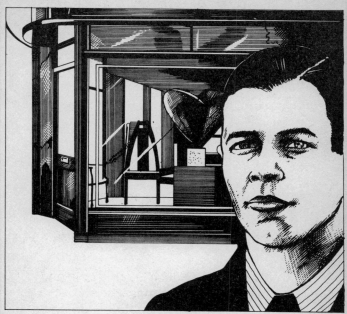

CAMDEN PASSAGE

Islington is beloved by the Man of Property. Its rows of Georgian residences of grey brick, white sash and bright door are very charming and convenient for the City. And then there's Sadler's Wells, the Screen on the Green, the Little Angel Marionette Theatre. And yet, the real impression of Islington is not its genteel, cultured facade but Upper street, wide-skirted, lorry-tramped, cheap varnished, where the joyless Hilda waits for the bus and the gritty wind tears at a poster for reduced mirrors. Islington has been coming up for years but has never quite made it. The antique stall and forlorn supermarket mingle with unease. Go to Camden Passage, browsers' and gourmets' delight, on Wednesdays and Saturdays when its pavements erupt into a market selling period clothes, clocks, general antiques, antiquarian books, Victoriana, and prints.

ANTIQUES

Strike One
51 Camden Passage, N1 (226 9709)
Mon-Sat 9.00am-5.00.
Where the cognoscenti buy time. Antique clocks, watches and barometers. Expensive but the service is excellent, including finding out of catalogue clocks and shipping worldwide.

BOOKS

The Angel Bookshop
102 Islington High St, N1 (226 2904)
Mon-Sat 9.30am-6.00.
Sitting at the mouth of Camden Passage, it is no hazard that this general bookshop slants towards antiques. Large range of paperbacks.

The Other Bookshop
328 Upper St, N1 (226 0571)
Mon-Sat 10.00am-6.00.
Alternative bookshop for the left-wing. Good selection of the literary politicos, feminism, sexual politics and anti-racism. Plus various angry newspapers, T-shirts and badges.

Sisterwrite
190 Upper St, N1 (226 9782)
Tue-Fri 11.00am-7.00, Sat 10.00am-6.00.
The fact and fiction of feminist writing and a good line in non-sexist kid's lit. Caustic posters, postcards and magazine of the cause.

CLOTHES

Call To Arms
79 Upper St, N1 (359 0501)
Mon-Sat 9.30am-5.30.
Shop gloomy with war relics. If you take it, general militaria, uniforms, flags, daggers, medals and all the other noises of war. You may also borrow the uniforms for theatrics and parties in their rapidly expanding hire section.

Clozo
1 Camden Walk, N1 (359 6474)
Mon-Sat 10.00am-6.00.
Apart from the bright new modernist labels and kooky spex, Clozo specialise in clothes between 1930 and the 60s depending on the retro swing. Clozo also make their own suits with original fabrics and have a good range of accessories, cufflinks, bow ties, braces and armbands.

The Greenery
24 Islington Green, N1 (359 8317)
Mon-Sat 9.00am-5.30, Thu 11.00am-3.00.
Airy wooden-floored space filled with period clothes from the turn of the century to the 40s, Victorian and Edwardian table linen and lace, stained glass lanterns and Julie Arkell silks.

Little Shoe Box
89 Holloway Rd, N1 (607 1247)
Mon-Sat 8.00am-6.00.
Made to measure shoe shop for pavement dazzlers. All styles from the simplest boot to the craziest creations in

Lurex, reptile, sequins, stiletto heel.

Rau
36 Islington Green, N1 (359 5337)
Wed & Sat 10.00am-6.00, Thu 11.00am-5.00.
Ethnic clothing at the other end from Carnaby Street's gaudy imitation. Original heavy embroidered dresses, gossamer-thin blouses from old silk saris, textiles from India and Afghanistan, saddlebags for cushions, silver amulets for wrists. Upstairs a selection of furniture — carved wooden chests, low chairs and lattice string beds.

FOOD

Chapel Street Market
Chapel St, N1.
Mon-Sun 8.00am-6.00.
Busy fruit and veg market selling most edibles from fresh dates to Cornish cabbage. Other stalls diversify into bed linen, cards, key cutting and at weekends, secondhand clothes.

Steve Hatt
88 Essex St, N1 (226 3963)
Tue-Sat 8.00am-5.15, Thu 8.00am-1.00.
The grand fishmonger of the North. Shiny spectrum of fish—coley to scotch salmon. Shellfish including live crabs, game and turkeys at Christmas. The traditional smoke hole at the back tempts with smoky, rich warm haddock, trout, mackerel and cod's roe. Resist not.

Rilla & Cox
5 Theberton St, N1 (354 2979)
Mon-Fri 9.00am-7.00,
Sat 10.00am-6.00. Sun 10.00am-1.00.
Small gourmet shop with a wide selection of over 50 cheeses, English pies, butter, croissants, frogs' legs, hams, jams and freshly ground coffees. Lazy epicures relish the ready-prepared dishes, boeuf bourgignon, civet de porc etc.

HOME

Argon
3 Theberton St, N1 (359 3845)
Mon-Sat 10.00am-5.30.
England's first gallery to exhibit exclusively the work of neon artists. Individual pieces and commercial examples are on display, together with over 300 slides. Commission yourself some electric art (neon poem, portrait or house number) and catch the light.

Cargo
296 Upper St, N1 (359 4281/226 7866)
Mon-Sat 10.30am-6.30.
Where the cane roams at large. Sells the essential paper lampshades, oatmeal bedspreads, mottled bamboo blinds, wicker baskets. Best for cheap dhurries and fishmongers plastic lobsters.

Geranium
121 Upper St, N1 (359 4281)
Mon-Sat 10.00am-6.00.
One more pine shop for the road. The old and the new is interspersed with bric-a-brac of the art deco sort and

ancient sewing machines.
Their pine stripping service
includes collection and
delivery. Throw away that
sandpaper.

Gill Wing
194/5 Upper St, N1 (359 7697)
Mon-Sat 10.00am-6.00.
*Brimming with local ceramics,
glass, cushions and
predictable gifts, cups with
legs and Crabtree & Evelyn
jams etc.*

Schram & Scheddle
262 Upper St, N1 (226 4166)
Mon-Sat 10.00am-5.00.
*Originally a photocopiers and
dyeline printers, this shop has
taken an innovative deviation
into 'preposterous presents'
from First World War
postcards from the trenches
and old magazines to flying
ducks and lazer specs.*

Smokes
204 Upper St, N1 (226 0226)
Mon-Sat 6.30am-7.00, Sun
7.00am-1.30.
*A brilliant selection of import
tobaccos, cigarettes, cigars
and cigarette papers. Smokers
haven with not a disapproving
look in sight. Also a sharp
source of graphics, postcards,
birthday cards etc.*

WHERE TO REST YOUR FEET

Roxy Diner
267 Upper St, N1
The northern burger.

Grapes Wine Bar
Angel Arcade, Camden
Passage, N1
Blackboard, wood, wine,

pepper steak, farmhouse soup
in a candle-spluttering
basement, laid back from the
antiques.

TRANSPORT

**(All details subject to change.
Phone 01-222 1234 at anytime,
day or night to check details.
Some routes shown do not
operate every day of the
week.)**

Tube: Angel, Highbury &
Islington
Buses: 4 (Mon-Sat only), 19,
30, 38, 43 (Mon-Sat
only), 73, 104
(everyday except
Mon-Fri evenings),
171, 172, 214, 277
(Mon-Sat only), 279
(Mon-Sat only), 279a
(Sun only)
Night: N96, N96

1. Strike One
2. The Angel Bookshop
3. The Other Bookshop
4. Sister Write
5. Call to Arms
6. Clozo
7. The Greenery
8. Little Shoe Box
9. Rau
10. Chapel Street Market
11. Steve Hatt
12. Rilla & Cox
13. Argon
14. Cargo
15. Geranium
16. Gill Wing
17. Schram & Schreddel
18. Smokes

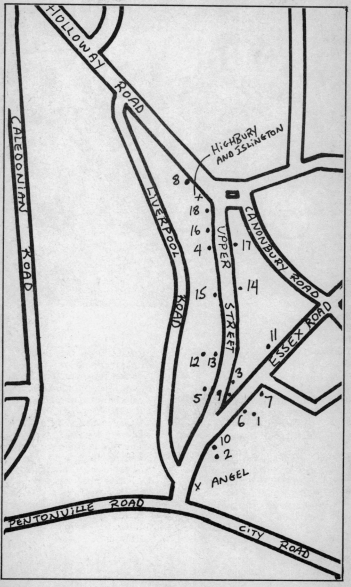

CAMDEN

CAMDEN LOCK

Camden, radical village, is where the alternative people moved in the 70s. Set between the dismal reality of Euston and King's Cross and the greener escape of Regent's Park, this is trendiland, bursting with workshops, old pine shops, cheap vegetable stalls and little Greek restaurants. In the streets the muesli children jostle with the bottle-swaggering down and outs and learn about Life. There are pubs where they sell Real Beer, cinemas that show the latest subtitles. Catch the Fringe at the Roundhouse, rhythm'n'booze at Dingwalls (free on Saturday lunchtimes), or rollerwhiz at the Electric Ballroom. At weekends the Lock Market bristles with stalls of bric-a-brac, old clothes, Edwardian bicycles and homemade jams. The no-nuke families go for walks along the canal and buy squidgy cake from a woman in fingerless gloves. Camden is never boring but by yoghurt, it's smug.

ANTIQUES

Gallerie 1900
267 Camden High St, NW1
(485 4955)
Mon-Sat 10.00am-6.00.
Concentrates on les Arts Nouveau and Deco from England and the Continent. Fine selection of the useful and decorative including rich-coloured geometric wall hangings, glass, pewter, coffee sets, jardinières, silver frames and bronze figures.

Odditys
72/73 Chalk Farm Rd, NW1
(263 9655)
Mon-Sat 10.00am-6.00.
Indoor market selling a wild variety from indoor bulbs to grow where there is little light to 30s ceramics, to the thin riveting borderline between junk and antiques.

BOOKS

Compendium
234 Camden High St, NW1
(485 8944/267 1525)
Mon-Sat 10.00am-6.00, Thu 11.00am-6.00.
Flagship of Camden and leading alternative bookstore. Apart from providing the word on solving the socio-psycho-religio-economic problems of this sad planet, Compendium imports a great deal of American literature which is otherwise unavailable in this country. See also for sections on contemporary music, the Occult and Feminism, for pamphlets and world wide mail order.

Primrose Hill Books
134 Regent's Park Rd, NW1
(586 2022)
Mon-Sat 10.00am-6.00.
Antiquarian and second-hand books for the curious and the collector.

CHILDREN

Humla
235 Camden High St, NW1
(267 7151)
Mon-Sat 10.00am-6.00.
Bright knitwear for children up to seven years (and a few for the envious adult too), clothes, books and toys.

Kristin Baybars
14 Inverness St, NW1 (485 1367)
Tue-Sun 10.00am-5.30.
Emporium of the tiny crafted toy. Miniatures for stockings, doll's houses, pockets and amazement. One of the few toyshops devoid of plastic.

Outgroans
190 Albany St, NW1 (387 2018)
Tue-Fri 10.00-5.00.
Second hand children's clothes to the age of twelve, especially anoraks, cardigans, dresses and babywear. Outgroans also sell end-of-lines and samples (Heals Jean Le Bourget) and customers' clothes (the standards are high), keeping them for two months and giving 50% of the selling price. Those eager to part with bags of outgrown clothes should go to the shop on Tue, Wed and Thu.

The Party Place
67/69 Gloucester Ave, NW1

(586 0169)
Tue-Sat 9.30am-5.30.
Everything you need for a party that throws jelly, bursts balloons and screams at Mr Punch. Over 30 different designs in paper tableware, cake decorations, crackers, masks, jokes, wrapping paper and all things for Halloween, Easter, Christmas and Valentine's Day.

CLOTHES

Formula
126 Regents Park Rd, NW1 (722 7955)
Mon-Sat 10.00am-6.00.
There are surprisingly few clothes shops in Camden. Stop here for cotton and corduroy utility wear and knitwear by French Connection, Strawberry Studio, Willi Wear, accessories and leather and suede which can be made to order.

Gohils Footwear
246 Camden High St, NW1 (485 9195)
Mon-Fri 9.00am-6.00, Thu 9.00am-1.00, Sat 9.00am-5.00, closed 12 noon-1.00.
Where the spirit of the clog flourishes on. Gohils hand-make leather boots and sandals, made to measure for awkward feet and undertake multifarious repairs, especially complicated ones.

Swanky Modes
106 Camden Rd, NW1 (485 3569)
Mon-Sat 10.00am-6.00.
For the ever-rolling new wave. Avant-garde

clothes and sharp retro accessories designed on the premises.

FOOD

Camden Wine and Cheese Centre
214 Camden High St, NW1 (485 5895)
Mon 10.00am-6.00 (wine only)
Tue-Fri 10.00am-5.30, Sat 10.00am-6.00, Sun 11.00am-4.00.
Fine wines and cheese collections from Austria to Australia. Star points are 50 champagnes at wholesale prices.

Chalk Farm Nutrition Centre
41/42 Chalk Farm Rd, NW1 (485 0116)
Mon-Sun 10.00am-7.00.
The ultimate expression of the brown rice philosophy, from sacks of grain to yoga for pregnancies. The shop is divided into sections, herbs, bread, homeopathic medicine etc and sells wholesome varieties of free range eggs, fresh goat's milk, organic fruit and veg, ginseng, royal jelly, vitamins, plants, skincare and beauty products and acupuncture.

The Greek Food Centre
12 Inverness St, NW1 (485 6544)
Mon-Sat 8.30am-6.00, Thu 8.30am-1.30.
Delicious Greek, Egyptian and Middle Eastern foodstuffs, including fresh vine leaves, dried fruit, Cypriot sausages, 52 different pastas and over 100 different herbs and spices.

Hare & Phoenix
16 Inverness St, NW1 (267 6586)
Mon-Fri 9.30am-6.30, closed Thu.
Profit sharing food shop whose bakery supplies 150 shops with rye and whole breads. Also sells five types of cheap coffee beans and sugar-free muesli.

Marine Ices
8 Haverstock Hill, NW3 (485 8898)
Mon-Sat 10.00am-11.00, Sun 11.00am-7.00.
Where to grab the decadent ice cream in small tubs or gallon hunks in all flavours, marsala, mango, peanut crunch, peppermint, melon, walnut etc. Also take away pizza and ice-cream cake to order.

HOME

Acquisitions
269 Camden High St, NW1 (485 4955)
Mon-Sat 10.00am-6.00.
Warm, glowing shop specialising in Victorian and Edwardian cast iron fireplaces and copies from original moulds, plus a myriad of fiery accessories such as coal buckets, bellows, fire irons, kettles and pokers. Also stocks gas coal effects for those who can't be bothered with fire lighters.

And So To Bed
6b Camden High St, NW1 (388 0364)
Mon-Sat 10.00am-6.00.
Weighty brass beds, plain, copied or with a dash of mother-of-pearl, headbeds, four posters, patchwork quilts and antique lace bedcovers. Here too a great assortment of wooden beds, panelled, carved, solid and sturdy-legged, perfect for the heavy Gothic sleeper. Also at 7 New Kings Rd, SW10.

Arlington Workshop
177 Arlington Rd, NW1 (485 0796)
Tue-Sat 10.00am-5.00.
Specialists in ceramics for plants of all kinds.

Blind Alley Ltd
Camden Lock, NW1 (485 8030)
Mon-Fri 9.30am-5.30, Sat 10.00am-5.30.
Tired of the swirling curtain? Take a blind, screen printed, air brushed or hand painted. Blinds here are also made to order and will be matched with the appointed room if possible.

Candles Shop
89 Parkway, NW1 (485 3232)
Mon-Sat 10.30am-6.00.
Light the way with candles of every colour and shape — delicious beeswax candles, dip-dye candles, candle holder, candles in the guise of mushrooms, Disney characters, political caricatures, skulls, candles smelling of fruit and flowers. Makes an amusing change from electricity. Also at 30 The Market, Covent Garden, WC2.

Casa Catalan
15/16 Chalk Farm Rd, NW1 (485 3975)
Mon-Sun 10.00am-6.00.
A breath of sunburst relief

from the relentless 19th Century shadows. Furniture from the patio, ceramic bird cages, hand-thrown terra cotta pots, plants, hand-painted umbrella stands plus the tile centre with over 2,000 tiles from Spain, Italy, France, Japan, Holland and England.

Chattels
53 Chalk Farm Rd, NW1 (267 0877)
Mon-Sun 12 noon-6.00.
What used to be a shop devoted to domestic and rural antiques has now been taken over by huge bunches of dried flowers, swinging in a faded and merry way from the ceiling. Also pot pourris and traditional baskets.

Colourspun
18 Camden Rd, NW1 (267 6317)
Tue-Sat 10.00am-5.30.
Yarn store who dye and spin their own multicoloured slub. Staider knits find handspun mohair, lopi for Icelandic jumpers, British sheep fleece and 66 Fair Isles (out of a potential 360) plus an assortment of needles, old buttons and plans for spinning and hand-knitting classes.

Richard Dare
93 Regent's Park Rd, NW1 (722 9428)
Mon-Fri 9.30am-6.00, Sat 10.00am-4.00.
Excellent kitchen shop, coffee grinders, copper saucepans, Sabatier knives. Best known for his French dinner services, Quimper, Gien and Luneville.

East Asia Company
103 Camden High St, NW1 (388 5783)
Mon-Sat 10.00am-6.00.
Eastern arts, crafts and publications. Where to get acupunctured.

Evans The Frame
71 Regent's Park Rd, NW1 (722 2009)
Mon-Fri 9.30am-6.00.
Framers with a choice of 250 frames. The shop also sells DIY frames, Hockney prints and dynamic postcards.

Kays Irish Music Centre
161 Arlington Rd, NW1 (485 4880)
Mon-Sat 10.30am-5.30, Sun 10.30am-1.30.
Though the main song is Irish Folk Music, there is also folk music of a more general tone and country and western. Stock selection of sheet music, records, cassettes, books and Irish jewellery. International mail order.

Kermessee
23 Camden Lock, Commercial Place, NW1 (267 1530)
Tue-Fri 10.00am-5.00, Sat-Sun 11.00am-5.30.
Camden is the land of stripped pine, this is therefore no surprise. Specialising in solid modern pine beds of the minimal design, space saving, bunks, with drawers, Kermessee also supply mattresses, chests, dressers and other wooden furniture.

Moorhouse Associates
240 Camden High St, NW1 (267 9714)
Mon-Sun 10.00am-6.00.

Designers and printers of materials for curtains and furniture with an aversion to 'anaemic florals'. If you want an alternative flapping at the window (ie bags of chips in uneasy colours) cut the cloth here. Moorhouse will design commissions and print to colours of your choice.

The Lock Shop
Commercial Place, Chalk Farm Rd, NW1 (485 3450)
Tue-Fri 11.00am-5.30, Sat-Sun 10.30am-6.00.
The place for hand-made British designs and crafts without craftiness. Good hunting ground for presents, witty knits, silk bow ties, clocks, swizzle sticks, silver jewellery, Edwardian peg dolls with china faces, glass geraniums, coloured glass and ceramic tiles.

Palmers
33/37 Parkway, NW1 (485 6163)
Mon-Sat 9.00am-6.00, Thu 9.00am-1.00.
Old-fashioned exotic pet shop famous since 1918 for their talking parrots and monkeys. Amongst the familiar gerbils and budgies find terrifying nine-foot pythons, tarantulas, a Red-Kneed Bird Eating spider, scorpions, lizards and tropical fish.

Patchwork Dog And Calico Cat
21 Chalk Farm Rd, NW1 (485 1239)
Tue-Sun 10.00am-6.00.
Formerly 21 Antiques, this shop still sells kitchen antiques, bottles to dressers, but now specialises in patchwork kits, fabrics, waddings, thread, books on the subject and antique quilts. They also run courses on patchwork and have a metals workshop for repairs in the basement.

Poster Shop
1 Chalk Farm Rd, NW1 (267 6985)
Tue-Fri 10.00am-6.00, Sat-Sun 10.30am-6.30.
Dedicated to rescuing the poster from its cultural bathos. Large selection of original posters, mostly commercial and theatrical. The Poster Shop also run a mounting and framing service not restricted to their posters.

Stove Shop
Camden Lock, Chalk Farm Rd, NW1 (969 9531)
Sat, Sun 11.00am-5.30 (weekdays by appointment)
Those averse to dull central heating can buy the alternative solid iron wood-fuelled stove here. Fully renovated to working order, the stoves are built for heating purposes but most have hot plates for kettles and the larger ones have ovens. From Britain, France, Norway and many from Denmark dating from 1870.

CAMDEN

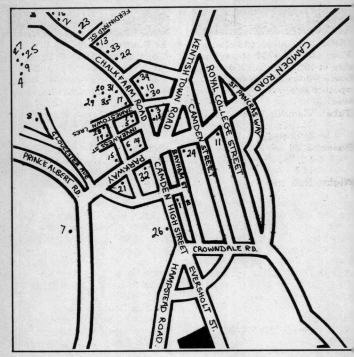

1. Gallerie 1900
2. Odditys
3. Compendium
4. Primrose Hill Books
5. Humla
6. Kristin Baybars
7. Outgroans
8. The Party Place
9. Formula
10. Gohils Footwear
11. Swanky Modes
12. Camden Wine and Cheese Centre
13. Chalk Farm Nutrition Centre
14. The Greek Food Centre
15. Hare & Phoenix
16. Marine Ices
17. Acquisitions
18. And So To Bed
19. Arlington Workshop
20. Blind Alley Limited
21. Candles Shop
22. Casa Catalan
23. Chattels
24. Colourspun
25. Richard Dare
26. East Asia Company
27. Evans the Frame
28. Kays Irish Music Centre
29. Kermessee
30. Moorhouse Associates
31. The Lock Shop
32. Palmers
33. Patchwork Dog and Calico Cat
34. Poster Shop
35. Stove Shop

114

CAMDEN

TRANSPORT

(All details subject to change. Phone 01-222 1234 at anytime, day or night to check details. Some routes shown do not operate every day of the week.)

Tube: Camden Town, Mornington Crescent (closed Sat & Sun)

Buses: 3, 24, 27, 29, 31, 46, 53, 68, 74, 134, 137, 214, 253

Night: N90, N93

WHERE TO REST YOUR FEET

Le Routier Cafe
Commercial Pl, Chalk Farm Rd, NW1
Camden Lock's excellent wine and bistro food, summer tables outside amongst the painterly mix of workshop and canal barges.

Splinters
232 Camden High St, NW1
Thick milkshakes, burgers (also to take away) and cocktails.

FLASK WALK

Hampstead was where the grand and 'artistic' escaped to have wild parties and grow their own vegetables when they had made money out of the swinging sixties. It is perched upon the hill like a castle protecting its borgeiousie, where the inhabitants talk of going into London as if it were some dangerous, far-off land. It's streets featured in countless English films and depressed women's fiction, have the postcard charm of a Sussex village, peppered with wine bar and some rich but dull dress shops. Don't look for adventure here. Go instead to the Heath, especially in summertime when you can listen to the orchestra play in the grounds of Kenwood House.

ANTIQUES

Hampstead Antiques Emporium
12 Heath St, NW3 (794 3202)
Tue-Sat 10.00am-6.00.
22 dealers gather in a cluster of buildings and sell a rich mixture of porcelain, metalware, glass, silver, watches and lamps.

H Knowles Brown
27 Hampstead High St, NW3 (435 4775)
Tue-Fri 9.00am-5.30, Sat 9.00am1.00.
Old fashioned jewellers with timbered ceiling and leaning towards clocks. Keep a look out for exhibitions of unusual clocks and modern jewellery. Repairs and insurance.

BOOKS

Keith Fawkes & Stanley Smith
13 Flask Walk, NW3 (435 0614)
Mon-Sun 10.00am-6.00.
Set amongst the pastel cottages and bijou restaurants, find this compulsive second hand and antiquarian bookshop. Buy and sell.

High Hill Bookshop
6 Hampstead High St, NW3 (435 2218)
Mon-Sat 9.30am-6.30.
Large general bookshop with comprehensive stock of hard and paperbacks.

CHILDREN

Fred Flintstone
16/18 Heath St, NW3 (435 9647)
Mon-Sat 9.30am-6.00.
Despite its cartoon name, children who hunt for clothes in this shop are not the sort who go climbing trees and chew gum. Here the child is a small adult and wears only dungarees of the cleverest cut in the right colours and takes a suit of swirl of gold and black for the evening. Designers include Daniel Hechter, Michael Leon, Pierre Cardin and Cacherel. Babywear begins at zero (knickerbockers from six months) and there is a shoes and accessories section, plus toys.

CLOTHES

Benetton
40 High St, NW3
(435 4669)
Mon-Sat 10.00am-6.00.
The northern outpost for the bright plain Italian knits.

Chic
74/82 Heath St, NW3 (435 5454)
Mon-Sat 9.30am-5.30.
Where to gather the top British designers, Bruce Oldfield, Jean Muir, Pauline Wynn Jones, John Bates and the younger talents of Jasper Conran and Wendy Dagworthy. No 74 for exclusive leather shoes, No 78 for silken lingerie and No 82 for clothes, especially for ball dresses. The service reflects the quality of the shop, a rare thing in a surly climate.

Hampstead Bazaar
30 Heath St, NW3 (431 3343)
Mon-Sat 10.00am-6.00.
Clothes of ethnic stitch (but not of the cheesecloth and kaftan variety) imported from France, Morocco and India. Best for antique fringed shawls, bright Eastern slippers, leather belts and handknits. Also at 6 Blenheim Crescent, W11.

Peace & Quiet
15 High St, NW3 (435 6969)
Mon-Sat 10.00am-6.00.
Retails in the main under its own label at virtually wholesale prices, mostly utility wear with some sharpcut leather and Fiorucci jeans. Good for accessories. Also under its wing is the shoe shop

Hobbs
9, High St, NW3 (431 2251)
Mon-Sat 10.00am-6.00.
for Italian boots and shoes. For other branches in this area check **Monsoon** *1 High St,* **Meenys** *30 High St and* **Jigsaw** *83 Heath St.*

FOOD

Community Centre Markets
78 Hampstead High St, NW3
Tue-Sat 10.00am-5.30.
Outside stalls brimming with fresh fruit, veg, fish, cheeses and pet food. On Sats an indoor market sells antiques, second hand books, herbs and wholefoods.

Elena
87 Heath St, NW3 (794 0798)
Mon-Wed 9.30am-5.30, Thu
9.30am-1.00, Fri 9.30am-5.30,
Sat 10.00am-6.00.
Cottagy chocolate shop decked with handmade Belgian downfalls, Fresh cream, liqueurs, truffles, pralines, sugared almonds in pink boxes.

Lodders at the Coffee and Tea Warehouse
2 Flask Walk, NW3 (435 0959)
Mon, Wed & Fri 9.30am-5.30,
Thu 9.30am-1.00, Sat
9.00am-6.00.
Small shop packed with freshly ground coffees and teas (including herbals, live yoghurts, wholemeal bakeries and holistic goodies, vitamins, natural cosmetics and over 100 different herbs and spices).

Rosslyn Hill Delicatessen
55 Rosslyn Hill, NW3
Tue-Sat 9.30am-6.30, Sun
9.30am-2.00.
Excellent Italian delicatessen swinging with numerous pastas, cheeses, smoked meats, olives etc, especially good for charcuterie, creme fraiche, smoked eel and duck, excellent French bread.

HOME

Culpeper
9 Flask Walk, NW3 (794 7263)
Mon-Sat 9.30am-6.00.
Herbalists offering every medicinal herb under the honest sun, plus natural cosmetics, bath salts, loofahs, pot pourris and herbal pillows. Mail order.

Cane & Table
36 Rosslyn Hill, NW3 (435 2431

Mon-Sat 10.00am-6.00.
Apart from reflecting its titles, Cane & Table have plants spilling on to the pavements, antique bamboo, hand painted tiles, natural beauty products, terracotta pots and wicker work.

Cucina
8 England's Lane, NW3 (722 7093)
Tue-Sat 10.00am-6.00.
Cooking crocks, raw Provencal pottery, traditional wooden games, baskets and bamboo, for home hunters and present hunters.

MAIDA VALE & KILBURN

Maida Vale, St John's Wood and its rougher edge Kilburn are mainly residential and abound in corner shops.

BOOKS

The Kilburn Bookshop
8 Kilburn Bridge NW6(328 7071)
Mon-Sat 9.30am-6.00.
Good general bookshop, specialising in feminism, alternative literature and Irish books.

Eric and Joan Stevens Booksellers
74 Fortune Green Rd, NW6 (435 7545)
Sats only 10.00 am-6.00.
Second hand bookshop with a good selection and friendly atmosphere. Buy and sell.

CLOTHES

Flak
134 West End Lane, NW6 (328 3495)
Mon-Fri 10.00am-7.00, Sat 10.00am-6.00.
Army surplus and work clothes store. Those deeply into the utilitarian chic take the Chino trousers, fatigues, khaki and camouflage, thick socks, thermal underwear, jungle boots and flying suits. The hats are good for showoffs. Hire service.

Viva
72 St John's Wood High St, NW8 (586 8600)
Mon-Sat 9.30am-6.00
One of the brighter surprises in this dinner party street. Classic and casual clothes of mainly French and Italian design for the richer North London taste. Labels include George Rech, Ventilo and Sportmax, shirts by Cacherel and children's clothes by Neuman.

FOOD

Ackerman's Chocolates
9 Goldhurst, NW6 (624 2742)
Mon-Fri 9.00am-6.00, Sat 9.00am-1.30
Excellent choc shop, selling the tempting stuff from Harrods to Macys. Tell the diet go hang and go wild about Champagne truffles, the chocolate zoo (cats to crocodiles), waferthin chocolate mints and oranges, noisettes, liquers and chocolate creams. Ackerman's kindly make special chocolates for diabetics. Also **Rilla & Co** *8 West Smithfield*

119

Alexis
272 West End Lane, NW6 (794 2617)
Mon-Sat 9.00am-6.00, Sun 9.00am-1.00
Continental bakery and patisserie. Specialises in fresh-cream gateaux and mouth-melting strudel. Where to grab the fresh yeast.

Osaka
17/17a Goldhurst Terrace, NW6 (624 4983)
Mon-Sat 8.00am-8.00, Sun 11.00am-7.00.
Specialist Eastern shop selling spices, Indian sweets, henna, grains and Oriental foodstuffs.

Superfoods
21/23 Clifton Rd, W9 (286 1668)
Mon-Sat 7.00am-7.00, Sun 7.00am-1.00.
Jewish delicatessen piled with the darker breads, smoked meats, pickles and a good selection of coffees.

Waitrose
John Barnes 199 Finchley Rd, NW3 (624 6000)
Mon 1.00-6.00, Tue-Wed 9.00am-6.00, Thu-Fri 9.00am-8.00, Sat 8.30am-4.00
A new and shiny food-factory with an excellent delicatessen (especially for an Eastern European palate) a patisserie piled with baroque Austrian pastry and a bakery selling 80 different kinds of bread, English cottage to the blackest rye (but get there early). Also fresh pasta and peppercorns and strange and exotic fruit and veg. with explanatory labels.

HOME

Bliss Chemists
54 Willesden Lane, NW6 (624 8000)
The 24 hour chemist of the North.

Clifton Nurseries
5a Clifton Villas, Warwick Ave, W9 (289 6851)
Mon-Sat 9.00am-6.00, Sun 10.30am-1.00.
London's favourite consumer garden. Large greenhouse for indoor plants, rocky outside for bedding plants, trees, herbs, stone statues, terracotta pots and compost. Good service. Also at The Colonnades, Bishops Bridge Rd, W2, and 16 Russell St, Covent Garden, WC2.

SPORTS

Beta Bikes
275 West End Lane, NW6 (794 4133)
Mon-Sat 9.00am-6.00, closed Thu, Sun 11.00am-1.00.
Good general bike store selling accessories and clothes, with repairs and hire service. Specialise in tandems.

1. Hampstead Antiques Emporium
2. H Knowles Brown
3. Keith Fawkes & Stanley Smith
4. High Hill Bookshop
5. Fred Flintstone
6. Benetton
7. Chic
8. Hampstead Bazaar
9. Peace and Quiet
10 Hobbs

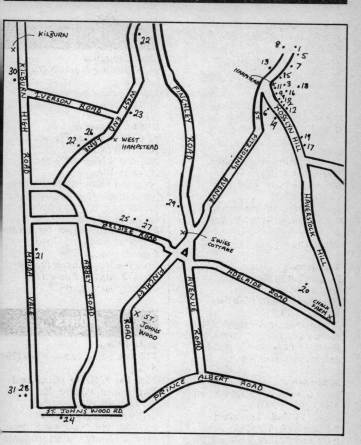

1. Monsoon
2. Meenys
3. Jigsaw
4. Community Centre
   Markets
5. Elena
6. Lodders at the Coffee
   and Tea Warehouse
7. Rosslyn Hill Delicatessen
8. Culpeper
9. Cane and Table
0. Cucina
1. The Kilburn Bookshop

22. Eric and Joan Stevens
    Booksellers
23. Flak
24. Viva
25. Ackermans Chocolates
26. Alexis
27. Osaka
28. Superfoods
29. Waitrose
30. Bliss Chemists
31. Clifton Nurseries
31. Beta Bikes

WHERE TO REST YOUR FEET

Hampstead is dotted with pink-washed pubs (try Flask Walk and environs). Otherwise:-

Peachey's
205 Haverstock Hill, NW3
Victorian, mirrored wine bar with seafish, game and chocolate cake on the good old days.

Louis
32 Heath St, NW3
Decadent Hungarian patisserie.

Warwick Castle
6 Warwick Pl, W9
Little Venice's beloved pub with home cooking and an almost on the canal charm.

TRANSPORT

(All details subject to change. Phone 01-222 1234 at anytime, day or night to check details. Some routes shown do not operate every day of the week.)

Tube: Warwick Avenue, Maida Vale, St John's Wood, Swiss Cottage, Belsize Park, Hampstead

Buses: 6, 8, 16, 16a daily, but not evenings or Sun), 46, 176

Night: N94 — to Maida Vale

Or: 2, 2b, 13, 31, 46 — to Finchley Road

Or: 24, 46, 268 — to Hampstead Heath

Or: 210, 268 — to Hampstead

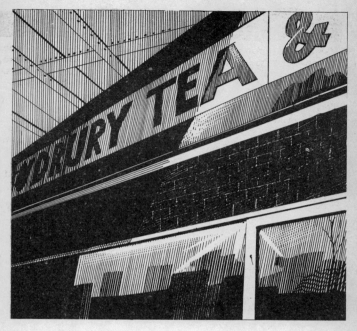

UNDERNEATH THE ARCHES

Southwark and beyond ends for most people at the grey matter of the South Bank and the Vics; sometimes on a brilliant day, it might begin again at Greenwich for a walk up to the observatory and a picnic on the meridian line. It is a desolate space, mashed by the planner and juggernaut and a poor shopping ground. At the western border, you may gather boxes of cabbage and cut flowers from vast New Covent Garden site (the rest from the giant Sainsbury's) and a new dog from the Battersea Dogs' Home. Architecture addicts stick close to Tower Bridge and Rotherhithe where the old warehouses of grim Dickensian brick and iron steps still fill the gritty air with the smell of spice and tea.

FOOD

Bottoms Up
Addington St, SE1 (633 0780)
Mon-Sat 9.30am-7.00, Sun 12
noon-2.00.
*Vast wine depot with some of
the sharpest prices in the city
— vodka to champagne.
Where the Beaujolais Nouveau
crowd grab it by the boxful.*

Drury Tea And Coffee Co 1-3
Mepham St, SE1 (928 2551)
Mon-Fri 8.30am-6.00. *Under
the arches of Waterloo Station
find this old fine coffee and
tea company who roast their
22 blends here, plus tea and a
large range of coffee
equipment.*

The Cut Market
Lower Marsh St, Waterloo Rd,
SE1. Mon-Fri 9.00am-5.00.
*Busy street market where the
Waterloo workers buy their
fruit and veg. Other food for
the basket (bread, fish) can be
found in shops lining the
route. See also*
East St Market *off Walworth
Rd, SE17, especially for plants.*

New Covent Garden
Nine Elms, Vauxhall, SW8 (720
2211) Mon-Sat 4.00-11.00am.
*Certainly not as romantic as it
used to be amid the cobbles of
the ancient regime but there's
definitely more space and
efficiency. The approach
seems more like an airport
than a fruit and flowers
market. You can enter as a
retailer if you buy in bulk (a
box full of lettuce, at least a
sack of potatoes) but don't be
surprised if a trader refuses to
serve you. Don't forget the
flower market for boxes of cut
flowers and giant palms.*

O Bellusci
39 South Lambeth Rd, SW8
(582 0766)
Mon-Sat 8.30am-7.00.
*Bright edible spark amidst the
grey. This English and
Continental deli stocks the
wide-swinging salami,
cheeses, green olive oils, fresh
ground coffee, pasta, coloured
tins, fruit and wines.*

Bob White
1 Kennington Lane, SE11 (735
1931) Tue-Fri 9.00am-5.00, Sat
8.30am-5.30, Sun 7.30am-5.00.
*Famous shellfish shop of the
South — lobsters, crabs,
cockles, mussels, winkles,
whelks etc in vast amounts
(watch out for the queues).
Most of the shellfish is cooked
on the premises (plus their
jellied eels) and they also stock
fresh fish and birds at
Christmas. Also stall at the
Oval on Sundays.*

HOME

Salvation Army
124 Spac Rd, SE16 (237 1107)
Mon-Fri 8.00am-12 noon,
1.00-3.30.
*Second-hand furniture. As
most of the stuff is donated to
the Army, it is mostly modern
and mostly nasty. But the
prices are very low and a
sharp-eyed hunt will not go
unrewarded.*

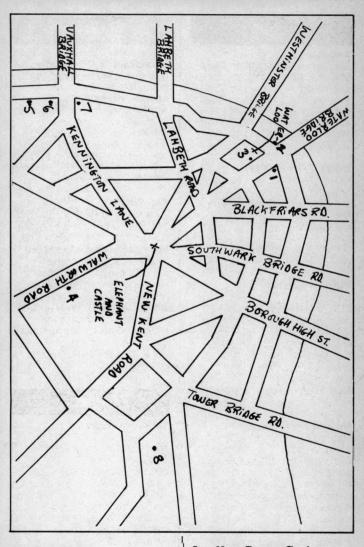

1.	Bottoms Up	5.	New Covent Garden
2.	Drury Tea and Coffee Co	6.	O Bellusci
3.	The Cut Market	7.	Bob White
4.	East Street Market	8.	Salvation Army

125

SOUTH OF THE RIVER EAST

WHERE TO REST YOUR FEET

The Archduke
Concert Hall Approach, SE1
Underneath the arches with bare brick and pimary pipes and jazz at night time. Good for a quick bottle and salad plate before or after a performance on the South Bank. Upstairs for sausages.

South of the Border
8 Joan St, SE1
Old factory converted to cocktails and cultural fodder. Roof garden, convenient for the Vics.

Young Vic Coffee Bar
66 The Cut, SE1
Wholesome fare for the bean brigade — flapjacks, pumpkins, beanshoots and soups on pine tables.

TRANSPORT

(All details subject to change. Phone 01-222 1234 at anytime, day or night to check details. Some routes shown do not operate every day of the week.)

Tube: Waterloo, Vauxhall, London Bridge, Elephant & Castle, Lambeth North, Oval

Buses: 5, 177, 501, 513, 18, 501, 513, 77, 77a, 168a, 76, 4, 68, 149, 168a, 171, 239, 42, 78, 35, 48, 95, 133, 109, 172, 184, 44, 88, 170, 507, 155, 8a, 10, 40, 44, 2, 2b, 36, 36a, 36b, 185, 159, 12, 53, 70, 1, 176, 21, 43, 47, 70, 188

BATTERSEA POWER STATION

South of the River (incorporating Clapham, Battersea, Barnes et al) is at most times accompanied by a sigh of consolation from those upon the Northern side. Just one bridge too far, they say. The reasons for the middle class migration across are simply those of finance, and though they may say it's quieter and greener and not really that much further if you think about it, save for the wondrous Battersea Power

Station it still has a dull suburban heart. In the bourgeois pockets that break the endless rows of Edwardian villas, find the excellent delicatessens, pine shops, period clothes shops, healthy, crafty shops and the occasional shop that, for a visitor, makes the trip worthwhile. Fine supermarkets and chain stores in Putney High Street and Wandsworth's Arndale Centre.

CLAPHAM

FOOD

Here Is Food
26 The Pavement, Clapham
Common, SW4 (622 6818)
Mon-Sun 10.00am-9.00.
*Home cook shop with food for
gifts and last fling dinner
parties. Fresh bread, free
range eggs, potted herbs,
jams and pickles.*

Rainbow Groceries
153 Clapham High St, SW4 (622
1230)
Mon-Thu 10.00am-5.30, Fri &
Sat 10.00am-6.00.
*Good wholefood shop with
own bakery tempting the
calories with pizzas, grainy
breads, carrot cake, flapjacks
etc plus the essential lentil,
vitamins and soya.*

BATTERSEA

CLOTHES

Glamour City
54 Battersea Bridge Rd, SW11
(223 7436)
Mon-Fri 10.00am-6.00, Sat
10.00am-5.00.
*Excellent period clothes shop,
specialising in the 50s. Silk
kimonos, party dresses,
wedding dresses, long gloves,
perching hats, dress suits,
drawers of lace and white
cloth and a very good
selection of jumpers, including
Arans. Unlike most original
clothes shops, this doesn't
have that weary 'Aladdin's*

*Cave' junkheap feeling,
instead it is graphically laid
out without sharktoothed
prices.*

George Malyard
137 Lavender Hill, SW11 (223
8292)
Tue-Sat 10.00am-5.30
*Great old-fashioned hat shop,
especially for trilbies,
homburgs and the summer
panama. Also makes to order.*

Thrift Shop
67 Falcon Rd, SW11 (228 2322)
Mon-Thu 10.00am-6.00. Wed
10.00am-1.00, Fri 10.00am-7.00,
Sat 10.00am-5.30.
*The Thrift Shop stocks most of
the secondhand hardy
perennials: jeans, fur coats,
basketball jackets, miniskirts
of suede and tartan, plus Fair
Isle and Aran sweaters, flannel
shirts, Fred Perrys, and
dresses, working and
flamboyant of decades 30, 40
and 50. Leather aficionados
take their main song, the
flying jacket, plain or painted;
heavies the German
trenchcoats.*

FOOD

Acquired Taste
9 Battersea Rise, SW11 (223
9942)
Mon-Sat 10.00am-9.00, Sun 12
noon-2.00.
*Cultivated delicatessen of the
backwoods, celebrating the
cheese in no mean way. Other
shelf temptations include
Jackson's teas, bottled fruits,
jams, good wine stock, real
beer, Loseley dairy products,
home made pates and herbs.*

Di's Larder
62 Lavender Hill, SW11 (223 4618)
Mon-Sat 10.00am-7.00.
Natural food store with the compulsory dried fruits, yoghurt, muesli and whole grains. The difference is in the bread counter with homemade granary, sesame, wholewheat, caraway and soda loaves.

Grocers
256 Battersea Rise, SW11 (223 9211)
Mon-Sat 10.00am-5.30.
Concept health food shop with green facade, dark wooden floor and huge jars of herbs and spices on the upper shelf. Keep fit with organic porridge, dried seaweed, sugarfree jams, wholewheat spaghetti, kelp and garlic pills, free range eggs and goat's milk. Hot soup also served.

J Mist & Sons
254 Battersea Park Rd, SW11 (228 6784)
Tue-Sat 7.30am-5.00, Wed 7.30am-12.30.
Lively fish shop with lobster nets swinging from the ceiling, also selling shellfish and trays of eggs.

HOME

Davy
3 Battersea Rise, SW11 (228 04664)
Mon-Sat 2.00-6.00, Thu 10.00am-2.00.
Old curiosity shop crammed with kitsch China, tins, buttons, bottles, hatpins, bookends, postcards and glass from dead parlours. A good place for magpies and present searchers.

WANDSWORTH

CHILDREN

The Rocking Horse
340 York Rd, SW18 (874 5291)
Mon-Sat 10.00am-5.00.
'Couture for the Better Dressed Child', includes Rocking Horse's own label of tough utility, party dress, and witty jumpers, plus Osh Kosh dungarees, chic cuts by Pierre Cardin, designs by the RCA, knitwear by the cooperative Bootstrap and Petit Bateau underwear. A bright new spark in a desolate place.

FOOD

La Ciocciara
54 Garratt Lane, SW18 (874 9529)
Mon-Fri 9.30am-8.00, Sat 9.30am-6.00, Sun 10.00am-1.00.
Beneath the chill concrete monster of the Arndale Centre find this Italian deli for homemade pasta, salamis and smoked meats, panetone and pastries, sacks of rice and coffee beans.

HOME

Kite & Balloon Co
613 Garratt Lane, SW18 (946 5962)
Mon-Sat 9.00am-6.00.
Specialist kite shop. Figurative geometric, fighters, acrobats, plus kits, books and a kite

hospital. Informed service. Also for boxes of plain and printed balloons, printing service and huge helium filled silvered beasts for celebrations.

PUTNEY

BOOKS

Cobb & Webb Bookshop
21 Lacy Rd, SW15 (789 8840)
Mon-Sat 10.30am-5.30.
General secondhand bookshop with postcards and large selection of paperbacks. Buy and sell.

CHILDREN

Domat Designs
3 Lacy Rd, SW15 (788 5715)
Mon-Sat 9.15am-5.30, closed for lunch 1.30-2.00.
Charming, chaotic toyshop bright with wooden toys, penny toys, farm animals, puppets and puzzles. Domat also design functional furniture, such as bunk beds, which can be seen in the back room. Also at 44 Turnham Green Terrace, W4.

CLOTHES

Jigsaw
114 Putney High St, SW15 (785 6731)
Mon-Sat 9.30am-6.00.
There are several clothes shops in this frenetic High Street though none of them exactly grab you by the chequebook. This shop is the best in the area, especially for utility clothes, plus French Connection and Fiorucci labels.

HOME

Cookmate Reject Kitchen Shop
118 High St, SW15
(788 1745)
Putney Bridge tube.
Mon-Sat 9.00am-5.30.
When Robert Carrier closed his two cookshops he sold his remaining stock to the ex-Ofram beginnings of the Reject Cookmate explosion. Now this chain of franchise winds its way round Britain and is still growing. This Putney branch sell the culinary bargain in the shape of glass, pine shelving, plainfaced china, cook's knives, director's chairs. The goods are sometimes slightly imperfect, bankrupt stock etc so are rarely innovative. Also at 119 Kings St, W6; Wood Green Shopping Centre, N22.

BARNES

CHILDREN

Sally Membery
1 Church Rd, SW13 (876 2910)
Mon-Sat 9.30am-6.00.
This shop make most of their own and will make to order. English style flourishes back in the nursery — sailor suits, silken party dresses, tartan and Liberty print day dresses with voile collars, Guernsey jumpers, duffle coats, Petit

Bateau underwear and soft Viyella check shirts.

Bennetts
63 Barnes High St, SW13
(878 5419)
Tue-Sat 9.00am-6.00.
General delicatessen with homebaked pies and witty sandwiches you may demolish at a bar.

Ferns
16 Barnes High St, SW13. (878 2468)
Mon-Sat 9.30am-5.30, Wed 9.30am-1.30.
Coffee specialists, Ferns also sell the machines, gift foods such as Provencal honeys and herbs, delicate biscuits, obscure marmalades and a wide range of chocolates and Jackson's teas.

Campion
71 White Hart Lane, SW13
(878 6688)
Mon-Sat 10.00am-6.00, closed 1.00-2.15.
Quirky gift/craft shop with a further room for exhibitions. The stock is not quite large enough to be compelling but scratch the surface and you will find Chinese boxes, Peruvian dolls' houses, illustrated books (especially children's), Virago publications, toys and candles.

The Body Shop
1a White Hart Lane, SW13
(876 1002)

Mon-Sat 10.00am1.00, 2.006.00.
The Southern branch of this highly successful vegetarian beauty shop where cost is cut by forgoing the packaging. The power of the name however is not forgot — Seaweed and Birch Shampoo, Goat's Milk with Honey Soap, Elderflower Eye Gel, Sunflower Night Cream, White Grape Skin Tonic etc. Plus natural sea sponges, honeybased leg wax, tiger balm, herb pillows, Elizabethan wash balls and Pot Pourri.

Yvonne Peters
17 Barnes High St, SW13.
(876 3775)
Mon-Sat 10.15am-5.30, closed Wed and 1.00-2.15 for lunch.
Small kitchen suppliers with some excellent English country baskets, mostly from the Manchester area, coffee machines, French coffee cups and white china, honey glazed earthenware dishes, recycled glass and Sabatier knives.

Peacock
3 White Hart Lane, SW13 (878 3012)
Mon-Fri 9.30am-5.30, Sat 9.30am-5.00.
Excellent interior design shop with wide ranging wallpapers, fabrics and paints and helpful staff. Names to splash your rooms with include Designers Guild, Osborne & Little and French designs.

RICHMOND

ANTIQUES

Mollie Evans
84 Hill Rise, Richmond, Surrey
(948 0182)
Tue-Sat 10.30am-5.30 (closed
Weds) Sun 2.305.30.
*Rural antiques of great bucolic
charm, quilts, pitchforks,
Victorian games, rockers.
Compulsive.*

BOOKS

Lion & Unicorn Bookshop
King St, Richmond, Surrey
(940 0483)
Mon-Sat 9.30am-5.30.
*Fine children's bookshop, fact
and fiction and especially
good for picture books. Adults
next door.*

Penguin Bookshop
10 Kings St, Richmond, Surrey
(940 1802)
Mon-Sat 9.30am-5.30, Fri
9.30am-8.00.
*The Southern paperback
depot. The full range of
Penguins, Puffins, Pelicans
plus some other paperbacks
and hardbacks in a Conran
grey, black and scarlet place.*

FOOD

Kramer
3 Duke St, Richmond, Surrey
(940 1844)
Mon-Sat 9.30am-6.00.
*Austrian bakery, specialising
in fresh cream gateaux (try the
Black Forest) and apple strudel.*

Richmond Hill Delicatessen
22 Richmond Hill, Richmond,
Surrey (940 3952)
Mon-Sat 10.00am-7.00.
*Narrow, woodlined, cheerful
shop with large variety of
cheeses, homecooked pates,
quiches, chickens, salads,
esoteric jams, fresh bread and
unusual teas.*

Richmond Tea and Coffee
9 Hill Rise, Richmond, Surrey
(940 0855)
Mon-Sat 9.00am-6.00, Wed
9.00am-1.00.
*Specialists of the bean and leaf
who byline in chocolates,
honeys and machines.*

CLAPHAM
1. Here is Food
2. Rainbow Groceries

BATTERSEA
3. Glamour City
4. George Malyard
5. Thrift Shop
6. Acquired Taste
7. Di's Larder
8. Grovers
9. J Mist & Sons
10. Davy

WANDSWORTH
11. The Rocking Horse
12. La Ciocciara
13. Kite & Balloon Co

PUTNEY
14. Domat Designs
15. Cobb & Webb Bookshop
16. Jigsaw
17. Cookmate Reject Kitchen
    Shop

BARNES
18. Sally Membery
19. Bennetts
20. Ferns

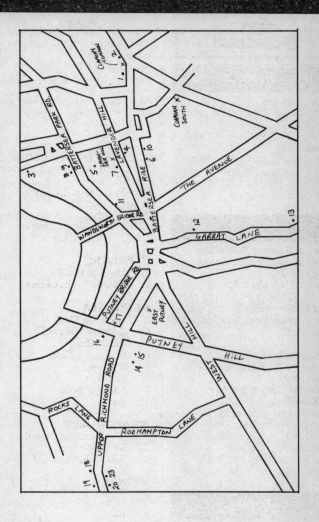

21. Campion
22. The Body Shop
23. Yvonne Peters
24. Peacock

RICHMOND
25. Mollie Evans

26. Lion & Unicorn Bookshop
27. Penguin Bookshop
28. Kramer
29. Richmond Hill Delicatessen
30. Richmond Tea and Coffee

SOUTH OF THE RIVER WEST

WHERE TO REST YOUR FEET

Clowns Cocktail Cafe
136 Upper Richmond Rd,
SW15
*Happy zappy little cocktail and
burger place, toy clowns,
waving greenery and light.*

Frogs Legs
264 Battersea Park Rd, SW11
*Wooden tables, wine,
changing bistro food, shadows
and friendly service.*

Original Maids of Honour
Kew Rd, Kew, Surrey
*Take a traditional English tea
after a walk through the
botanical splendour of Kew
Gardens.*

TRANSPORT

(All details subject to change.
Phone 01-222 1234 at anytime,
day or night to check details.

Some routes shown do not
operate every day of the
week.)

Tube: East Putney,
Richmond, Clapham
Common
Buses: 14, 22, 30, 37, 39, 74,
85, 93 — to Putney
(High St)
Or: 33 (Mon-Sat only), 37,
72, 73 (Sun only) — to
Barnes
Or: 7, 27, 33 (Mon-Sat
only), 37, 65, 73 (Sun
only), 290 — to
Richmond
Or: 19, 28, 39, 44, 77a, 170
(Mon-Sat only), 220,
249
Night: N68, N88 — to
Wandsworth
Or: 19, 39, 44, 45, 49, 170
(Mon-Sat only)
Night: N88 — to Battersea
Or: 35, 37, 88, 137, 155
(Mon-Sat only)
Night: N81, N87 — to
Clapham

134

A GUIDE TO

London's BEST Shops

PART II

PRODUCT SECTION

ANTIQUES

ANTIQUES

Antiques are in the eyes and purses of the beholder. Some buy for beauty, some for collections. others for investment. Whatever the vision, this city will realise it. London's antique dealers are too numerous to mention but here are some guidelines. The antique streets are:-
King's Road
for furniture from 18th Century mahogany to pine stripped from the 19th especially beyond the World's End (see also the Chenil Galleries, Chelsea Antique Market, Antiquarius)
Kensington Church Street *for the best in pottery and porcelain, some good period furniture and glass (see also Antique Hypermarket);*
Camden Passage *for the decorative, Victoriana and period clothes (Weds and Sats).* **Westbourne Grove** *for lesser furniture and lighting, mostly 19th C and* **Ledbury Road** *for prints (see also Portobello Market);* **Bond Street, Burlington Arcade** *(see also Grays Antique Market), plus* **Halkin Arcade** *for art nouveau and Art Deco and* **Knightsbridge Pavilion,** Brompton Rd, SW1.
Bermondsey Market Abbey St, SE1 *Friday mornings from dawn for the seething antique trade market. Not unlike Crewe Station where pieces fly in, change hands and head off to different stalls and shops. Sharp trained hawk-eyes may find a bargain, otherwise drink in the smoky,*

clattering chattering atmosphere.

ANTIQUITIES

Charles Ede
37 Brook St,W1 (493 4944)
Green Park tube.
Tue-Fri 12.30-4.30
Pre-classical and Coptic art (Eygptian, Greek, Roman, Persian)

ARCHITECTURAL

Crowther & Son
283 North End Rd, SW6
Fulham Broadway tube.
Mon-Fri 9.00am-6.00.
Rooms piled and shuttered with 18th C wood panelling, marble and wood carved chimney pieces, wrought iron and stone garden furniture and statues.

J Crotty & Son
74 New King's Rd, SW6 (385 1789) Parsons Green tube.
Mon-Fri 10.00am-5.00, Sat 10.00am-12.00 noon
19th and 20th C French and English fireplaces, grates and fire irons.

ART NOUVEAU/ DECO

Chiu
Halkin Arcade, W1
(235 5552) Knightsbridge tube.
Mon-Fri 10.00am-5.30, Sat 10.00am-1.00
Specialists in drawings and paintings 1875 to 1940, amid expanded metal walls revealing glass shelves of

*bronze and vase, black floor
and a maze of tiny spotlights.*

Chenil Galleries
181 King's Rd, SW3 (351 1145)
Sloane Sq tube.
Mon-Sat 10.00am-6.00
*Chenil has a broad selection of
antiques, but is strongly
defined by art nouveau and
deco design, glass, furniture,
ceramics, Lalique, Hoffmann.*

CARPETS

Benardout and Benardout
7 Thurloe Pl, SW7 (584 7658)
South Kensington tube.
Mon-Fri 9.00am-5.30, Sat
9.00am-12.30
Persian carpets and rugs.

C John
70 South Audley St, W1 (493
5288) Green Park tube.
Mon-Fri 9.15am-5.00
*Rare Oriental rugs, carpets
and tapestries.*

CHANDELIERS

Crick
166 Kensington Church St, W8
(229 1338) Notting Hill Gate
tube.
By appt advisable
*Where to swing the
chandelier, glittering in cut-
glass and ormulu. Of strange
and eccentric temperament.*

CLOCKS

E Hollander
80 Fulham Rd, SW3 (589 7239)
South Kensington tube.
Mon-Fri 9.30am-5.30

*Specialists in the English long-
case and bracket clock,
barometers and repairs.*

Ronald A Lee
1-9 Bruton Pl, W1 (629 5600)
Oxford Circus tube.
Mon-Fri 10.00am-5.00
*17th and 18th C English
clocks.*

COINS

Spink
517 King St, SW1 (930 7888)
Green Park tube.
Mon-Fri 9.30am-5.30
*Foremost coin and medal
dealers, worldwide
decorations, campaign medals,
Greek to English coins.*

FURNITURE

Mallet
40 New Bond St, W1 (499
7411) Bond St tube.
Mon-Fri 9.15am-5.15
*Large, expensive collection of
fine English furniture, mostly
18th C.*

Pelham Galleries
163/5 Fulham Rd, SW3 (589
2686) South Kensington tube.
Mon-Fri 9.00am-5.30, Sat
9.00am-1.00
*Good for large 18th C and
early 19th C pieces
(sideboards to carve mightily
upon, tables to dine from).*

John Keil
154 Brompton Rd, SW3 (589
6454) Knightsbridge tube
Mon-Fri 9.00am-6.00
*17th to 19th C English
furniture.*

137

ANTIQUES

Just Desks
20 Church St, NW8 (723 7976)
Edgware Rd tube.
Mon-Sat 9.30am-6.00
*Period and reproduction desk
chairs, writing tables and
filing cabinets.*

GLASS

Delomosne
4 Campden Hill Rd, W8 (937
1804) Notting Hill Gate tube.
Mon-Fri 9.00am-5.30, Sat
9.00am-1.00
*Fine collection of 18th and
early 19th C English and Irish
glass.*

W G T Burne
11 Eystan Pl, SW3 (589 6074)
Mon-Fri 9.30am-5.00, Sat
9.30am-1.00
*17th and 18th C wine glasses.
Plus cut glass, chandeliers and
paperweights. Repairs.*

Eric Lineham
62 Kensington Church St, W8
(937 9650) Notting Hill Gate
tube.
Mon-Fri 9.30am-5.30
*Specialise in English and
French art glass, cameo,
coloured Victorian.*

METALS

Robert Preston
121 Kensington Church St, W8
(727 4872) Notting Hill Gate
tube.
Mon-Fri 9.30am-6.00
*19th C brass and copper
(kettles, fenders), some
pewter. See also* **The Brass
Shop** *23 Pembridge Rd, W11
W11.*

Jeremy Cooper
9 Galen Pl, WC1 (242 5138)
Tottenham Court Rd tube.
Mon-Fri 10.00am-6.00, Sat
10.00am-2.00
Victorian bronzes.

ORIENTAL

Bluett
48 Davies St, W1 (629 4018)
Mon-Fri 9.30am-5.30
Bond St tube
*Early Oriental ceramics,
bronzes and jades.*

Eskenazi
Foxglove House, 166
Piccadilly, W1 (493 5464)
Piccadilly Circus tube.
Mon-Fri 10.00am-6.00
*Early Chinese works of art,
bronzes, Japanese lacquer, and
netsuke.*

Sparks
128 Mount St, W1 (499 2265)
Oxford Circus tube.
Mon-Fri 9.30am-5.00.
*Chinese works of art,
porcelain to screens.
See also* **Tempus Antiques** *43,
Kensington Church St, W8*

POTTERY & PORCELAIN

China Choice
7 New Cavendish St, W1 (935
0184) Bond St tube
Mon-Fri 10.00am-5.00, Sat
10.00am-1.00
18th C English porcelain.

Graham & Oxley
101 Kensington Church St, W8
(229 1850) Notting Hill tube

Mon-Sat 10.00am-5.30

ANTIQUES & ACQUISITIONS

Jean Sewell
3 Campden St, W8 (727 3122)
Notting Hill Gate tube.
Mon-Sat 10.00am-5.30
*Large, fine selection of antique
pottery and porcelain, 18th
and 19th C English tableware.
See also* **Mercury Antiques** *1
Ladbroke Grove, W11 for
ceramics.*

SILVER

S J Philips
139 New Bond St, W1 (629
6261) Bond St tube.
Mon-Fri 10.00am-5.00.
*Important, expensive
Continental and English
pieces.*

**Silver Vaults Chancery
House**
53/63 Chancery Lane, WC2
(242 3844) Chancery Lane
tube.
Mon-Fri 9.00am-5.30, Sat
9.00am-12.30
*Huge underground range of
silver, antique, second-hand
and new from 25 dealers.*

S J Shrubsole
43 Museum St, WC1 (405 2712)
Tottenham Court Rd tube.
Mon-Fri 9.00am-5.30
*18th C and Victorian British
silver, specialists in Sheffield
plate.*

J H Bourdon-Smith
24 Mason's Yard, Duke St, W1
(839 4714) Bond St tube.
Mon-Fri 9.30am-6.00
Georgian and Victorian silver.

TEXTILES

Mayorcas
38 Jermyn St, SW1 (629 4195)
Piccadilly Circus tube.
Mon-Fri 9.00am-5.30, Sat
9.00am-12 noon
*European textiles, tapestries,
damasks, embroideries, early
costume and painted fabrics.
See also* **Grays Antique
Market** *and* **Grays in the
Mews.**

ACQUISITIONS

*This section includes those
shops that specialise in old
and beautiful things that skirt
the edges of the antiques
market. For collectors and the
curious and the present
seekers. For general shops
that hoard the unusual, seek
out* **Stephen Long** *348 Fulham
Rd, SW6 (352 8226) and* **Loot**
*76/78 Pimlico Rd, SW1 Mon-
Sat 9.00am-6.00 (ring to check;
other times by appt)
Juke boxes from the time
when they were not just a row
of buttons set in pub formica.
Here they have the old style
mixed with old pinball
machines and football tables.
Prices according to the stage
of reconditioning.*

DOLLS

Kaye Desmond
17 Kensington Church Walk,
W8 (937 2602) Kensington
High St tube
Sats only 11.00am-3.00.
*Huge pre-1920 doll collection
mostly French and German.*

The Doll Shop
18 Richmond Hill, Richmond,

Surrey (940 6774) Richmond tube.By appt.
Antique dolls with waxen faces in their original party clothes. If they've lost them on the journey the costumes are carefully reproduced in old fabrics, even to the bonnet and shoes.

JEWELLERY

Big-time jewellery is found in Bond Street and Mayfair, the rocks in Hatton Garden, but intelligent modern stuff is hard to find.

Electrum Gallery
21 South, Molton St, W1 (629 6325) Bond St tube.
Mon-Fri 10.00am-6.00, Sat 10.00am-1.00
Where the most exciting and innovative work of contemporary designers sparkles and shines and jewellery is more an art than an accessory. Figurative to Futurist. Good service.

Nigel Milne
91 Mount St, W1 (493 9646) Green Park tube.
Mon-Fri 9.30am-6.00, Sat 10.30am-3.00
Bright and antique Edwardian and art nouveau jewellery.

JUKE BOXES

R G Edwards Amusement Machines
108 Thornton Rd, Thornton Heath, Surrey (684 6239)
Thornton Heath BR.
Mon-Sat 9.00am-6.00
Juke boxes from the time

when they were not just a row of buttons set in pub formica. Here they have the old style jukes mixed with old pinball machines and football tables. Prices according to the stage of reconditioning.

MUSIC BOXES

Keith Harding
93 Hornsey Rd, N7 (607 6181) Finsbury Park tube.
Mon-Fri 9.00am-6.00. Sat by appt.
Rooms piled with musical boxes. Restoration service and books on mechanicals.

PENS

Old fountain pens may be found in Portobello Market and Antequarius, King's Road. Also a small selection at **Paul Smith**, *44 Floral St, WC2. Otherwise try:*

The Pen Friend
7-8 Newbury St, EC1 (406 6542) Barbican tube.
Mon-Sat 9.00am-3.00
All designs from early tortoiseshell to latest metallics. Inks, nibs, holders and repairs.

Philip Poole
182 Drury Lane, WC2 (405 7097) Covent Garden tube.
Mon-Fri 9.00am-5.30
Where to find the nib in its now-meagre variety, plus quill pens, cutters, blotters and inkwells.

ACQUISITIONS

RAILWAYS

Collector's Corner
Cardington St, NW1 (387 9400/2537) Euston tube.
Mon-Fri 9.00am-5.00, Sat 9.00am-4.30
British Rail's nostalgia store, aptly sited near Euston Station. Station signs, bits of train and signalling equipment, clocks, crocks, enamelled badges, driver's badges, timetables and photographs.

RUGS

The Rug Shop
10 Eccleston St, SW1 (584 8724) Victoria tube.
Mon 2.00-6.00 Thu-Fri 10.00am-6.00, Sat 10.00am-1.00
Intricate Eastern floor and wall carpets. Specialists of the Kelim, the Rug Shop also make up cushions and ottomans from storage and saddle bags.

SHELLS

Eaton's Shell Shop
16 Manette W1 (437 9391)
Tottenham Ct Rd tube. Mon-Fri 9.30am-4.45, Sat 11.00am-3.00.
Seashells by their myriad selves, corals, shell jewellery, bamboo upstairs.

Precioushells
2a Vant Rd, Tooting, SW17 (767 5265) Tooting tube.
Mon-Fri 9.30am-5.00, closed Wed, Sat 9.30am-4.00
Seashells by their myraid selves, corals, shell jewellery pix, toys etc.

STAMPS & EPHEMERA

Harris Publications
42 Maiden Lane, WC2 (240 2286) Charing Cross tube.
Mon-Fri 9.00am-5.15, Sat 9.00am-1.00
Stamp collectors equipment — tweezers to magazines.

Royal Stamp Co
41/2 Bedford St, WC2 (836 6122) Charing Cross tube.
Mon-Fri 9.00am-5.30, Sat 9.30am-1.00
For world wide collectors, especially Great Britain's.

Pleasures of Past Times
11 Cecil Court, WC2 (836 1142) Leicester Sq tube.
Mon-Fri 11.00am-2.15, 3.15-6.00
Set amongst the bookshops, scraps and printed matter to delight a nostalgic's fluttering heart.

Quadrille Antiques
27 Craven Terr, W2 (262 7824) Lancaster Gate tube.
Tue-Sat 11.00am-6.00
Unusual ephemera shop, specialising in music covers, theatrical items and Valentines.

Robert Heron
46 The Market, Covent Garden, WC2 (379 7779) Covent Garden tube.
Mon-Sat 10.00am-8.00.
Specialists in early and rare English, French and American newpapers.

ART GALLERIES

VICTORIANA

Bayly's Gallery
8 Princess Arcade, (734 0180)
Piccadilly Circus tube.
Mon- Fri 10.00am-5.00.
*Unexpected shop in this dull
little arcade. Delicious
Victoriana, occasional
furniture and lamps upstairs,
downstairs for glass fruit
domes, china figures, tartan
boxes, teddy bears and a fine
collection of music hall
programmes, songs and
Valentines.*

WINE & ACCESSORIES

Richard Kihl
164 Regent's Park Rd, NW1
(586 3838) Chalk Farm tube.
Tues-Fri 9.30am-5.00, Sat
11.00am-5.00.
*Where the drinking
collectors reach for their claret
jugs and corkscrews. Fine
selection of old bottles,
decanters and glass.*

ART GALLERIES

OLD MASTERS

Abbott & Holder
75 Castelnau, SW13 (748 2416)
Hammersmith tube.
Sat 9.00am-5.00, other times by
appt.
*Light private house filled with
18th to 20th C watercolours
and drawings.*

Thomas Agnew
43 Old Bond St, W1 (629 6176)
Green Park tube.
Mon-Fri 9.30am-5.30, Thu
9.30am-7.00.
*Where the grand old masters
roost, oils and engravings of
high import.*

Basket & Day
173 New Bond St, W1 (629
2991) Green Park tube
Mon-Fri 9.30am-5.30.
*Early English and Old Master
drawings and prints.*

Browse & Darby
19 Cork St, W1 (734 7984)
Green Park tube.
Mon-Fri 10.00am-5.30, Sat
10.00am-12.30.
*19th and 20th C drawings and
sculpture of excellence.*

Colnaghi
14 Old Bond St, W1 (491 7408)
Green Park tube
Mon-Fri 9.30am-6.00, Sat
10.00am-1.00.
*Old powerful gallery for Old
Masters and drawings,
Oriental and Indian art.*

Covent Garden Gallery
20 Russell St, WC2 (836 1139)
Covent Garden tube.
Mon-Fri 10.00am-5.30, Sat
10.00am-12 noon.
*18th and 19th C oils,
watercolours and drawings,
English school, leaning
towards the literary and
architectural.*

Craddock & Bernard
32 Museum St, WC1 (636 3937)
Tottenham Court Rd tube.
Mon-Fri 9.30am-5.30.
*In the land of Bloomsbury,
darkly academic with a slight
eccentric creak, this gallery is
happy amongst the bookshops.
Fine old prints, Old Master to*

ART GALLERIES

Modern, etchings, lithographs, woodcuts.

Robert Douwma
93 Great Russell St, WC1 (636 4895) Tottenham Court Rd tube.
Mon-Fri 9.30am-6.00, Sat 10.00am-1.00.
Vast and good stock of antique maps, illustrated books, caricature, natural history.

Fine Art Society
148 New Bond St, W1 (629 5116) Green Park tube.
Mon-Fri 9.30am-5.30, Sat 10.00am-1.00.
19th and 20th C British Art, arts, fine and applied, including architectural drawings, costume design, Scottish canvas.

Grosvenor Gallery
48 South Molton St, W1 (629 0891) Bond St tube.
Mon-Fri 10.00am-6.00.
Agents for Erte, this gallery also stocks Russian Constructivists, Italian Futurists, Art Deco and Art Nouveau.

Haslitt, Gooden & Fox
4 Ryder St, SW1 (930 6821) Green Park tube
Mon-Sat 10.00am-5.30.
Specialises in French and English 18th and 19th C paintings and drawings.

Richard Kruml
47 Albermarle St, W1 (629 3017) Green Park tube.
Mon-Fri 11.00am-5.00.
Japanese prints.

Leggatt
30 St James St, SW1 (930 3772)
Green Park tube.
Mon-Fri 9.30am-5.00.
Grand gallery of the Old Masters in oils, English school.

J S Maas
15a Clifford St, W1 (734 2302) Bond St tube.
Mon-Fri 10.00am-5.00.
Victorian and pre-Raphaelite paintings, drawings and watercolours.

Christopher Mendez
51 Lexington St, W1 (734 2385) Oxford Circus tube
Mon-Fri 10.00am-5.00.
Master engravings, woodcuts and etchings.

The Parker Gallery
2 Albermarle St, W1 (499 5906) Green Park tube.
Mon-Fri 9.30am-6.00.
Nautical, military, sporting, topographical prints and paintings.

Spink
5/7 King's St, SW1 (930 7888) Green Park tube.
Mon-Fri 9.30am-5.30.
Vast and global art company. Old Masters, sculpture, English paintings and drawings, Orientals.

Louise Whitford
25a Lowndes St, SW1 (235 3155) Knightsbridge tube
Mon-Fri 10.00am-6.30
Home of Belle Epoque, Symbolists and Australians.

Christopher Wood
15 Motcomb St, SW1 (235 9141) Knightsbridge tube
Mon-Fri 9.30am-6.00.
High Victorian Art, pottery, photographs and sculpture.

ART GALLERIES

Plus: **Christopher Gibbs** 118 New Bond St, W1 and **Gooden & Fox** 38 Bury St, SW1 for Old Masters. **Lefevre** 30 Bruton St, W1 for French Impressionists, **Julian Hartnoll** 14 Mason's Yard, SW1 and **Hobhouse & Eyre** 39 Duke St, SW1 for pre-Raphaelites, **Fischer Fine Art** 30 King St, SW1 and **Achim Moeller** 8 Grosvenor St, W1 for German Expressionists.

MODERN & CONTEMPORARY

Curwen Gallery
1 Colville Place, Whitfield St, W1 (636 1459)
Warren St tube.
Mon-Fri 10.30am-5.00.
Mainly graphics of the contemporary sort. The Curwen Press also publish Hepworth, Piper, Frink and Henry Moore lithographs.

Anthony D'Offay
9 and 23 Dering St, W1 (629 1578) Bond St tube.
Mon-Fri 10.00am-5.30, Sat 10.00am-1.00.
No 9 for historical, principally British works, eg Bloomsbury. The newer space at no 23 is to show substantial artists from Europe and the United States, especially the latest concepts of Andre Long and Joseph Beuys.

Angela Flowers
11 Tottenham Mews, W1 (637 3089) Goodge St tube.
Tue-Fri 9.30am-5.30.
Small unrigid gallery of the multi-media especially the graphic and the photographic with Boyd & Evans, John Loker, Ian Breakwell and

Patrick Hughes, man of many rainbows. Excellent postcards.

Crane Kalman
178 Brompton Rd, SW3 (584 7566) Knightsbridge tube.
Mon-Fri 10.00am-6.00, Sat 10.00am-4.00.
Selective of the distinctive. Mainly 20th C greats such as Nicholson, Sutherland, Bacon and the later talents of Mary Newcomb. See also at 321 King's Rd, SW3 (352 5857) for 19th C paintings, mostly English and witty contemporaries.

Knoedler Kasmin
22 Cork St, W1 (439 1096)
Piccadilly tube.
Mon-Fri 10.00am-5.30, Sat 10.00am-1.00.
For the master whizz-kids: Stella, Frankenhaler, Kitaj, Caro, Lichtenstein and Hockney.

Francis Kyle
9 Maddox St, W1 (499 6870)
Oxford Circus tube.
Mon-Fri 10.00am-6.00, Sat 11.00am-5.00.
Sharp-witted gallery for the bright and decorative: Adrian George, Boyd Harte, Gerald Mynott; on the darker side, Edward Gorey, John Glashna and the literary canvas of Philip Core. Collectable posters in excellent taste.

Maclean Gallery
35 St George St, W1 (493 4756)
Oxford Circus tube
Mon-Fri 10.00am-5.30, Sat 10.00am-1.00 (during exhibitions
Sympathetic eye for the 20th C British Art: Sickert, Burra, Augustus and Gwen John, Roberts and the Vorticists.

ART GALLERIES

Bernard Jacobson
3 Mill St, W1 (439 8355) Oxford
Circus tube.
Mon-Fri 10.00am-6.00, Sat
10.00am-12 noon.
*British and American paintings
and prints. Innovators such as
Frank Auerbach, Robyn
Denny, Richard Smit and
Howard Hodgkin.*

Juda Rowan
11 Tottenham Mews, W1 (637
5517) Goodge St tube.
Mon-Fri 10.00am-6.00, Sat
10.00am-1.00.
*New British (Tim Head,
Anthony Green) and the
Russian constructivists.*

Piccadilly Gallery
16 Cork St, W1 (629 2875)
Green Park tube.
Mon-Fri 10.00am-5.30, Sat
10.00am-12.30.
*Symbolist stock, Eric Gill,
Stanley Spencer and
contemporary figurative and
ruralist painters (Graham
Ovenden, David Tindle).*

Photographers Gallery
5 Great Newport St, W1 (240
1969) Leicester Sq tube.
Mon-Sat 11.00am-7.00, Sun 12
noon-6.00.
*The photograph gallery —
photo-journalism, landscape,
commercial. Exhibitions of
Victorians to avant grade.*

Lisson Gallery
56 Whitfield St, W1 (631 0941)
Goodge St tube.
Mon-Fri 10.00am-6.00, Sat
10.00am-1.00.
*The international avant garde
concepts, including Sol Lewitt,
Richard Long, Donald Judd.*

Thumb Gallery
20/21 D'Arblay St, W1 (434
2931) Oxford Circus tube.
Mon-Fri 10.00am-6.00, Sat
11.00am-4.00.
*Graphics gallery with slick
emphasis on contemporary
prints. Works by food artist
Chloe Cheese, Andrew
Holmes, Sue Coe.*

Waddington Galleries
2, 31 and 34 Cork St, W1 (439
1866) Bond St tube.
Mon-Fri 10.00am-5.30, Sat
10.00am-1.00.
*High visible success from the
European greats to British
moderns, Peter Blake,
Hodgkin, Caulfield, Allan
Jones: no 2 for the moderns,
no 31 for graphics and
photography, no 34 for the
contemporaries.*

See also **Theo Waddington** at no
25 for Matisse to Eskimo art.
Plus **Nicola Jacobs** 9 Cork St
for new British abstracts,
Illustrators Art 16a D'Arblay
St, W1 for illustration
especially for children's
books, **Anthony Stokes** 3
Langley Court, WC2 for
strong British visuals (Glen
Baxter, Simon Read, Fay
Godwin), **Gimpel Fils** 30
Davies St, W1 for established
British, Europan and
American contemporaries
(Hepworth Davies).

ART & CRAFT SUPPLIES

Beatties
112 High Holborn, WC1 (405
6285) Holborn tube.
Mon 10.00am-6.00, Tue-Sat
9.00am-6.00.

145

Home of the model makers. Cars, planes, buildings and a great many trains. Meccano and a second-hand department.

JW Bollom
107 Long Acre, WC2 (836 3727) Covent Garden tube. Mon-Sat 9.00am-5.30.
The London Graphics branch, with a wide variety of artist's materials, Letraset and drawing as well as architectural furniture and equipment. Also at 15 Theobalds Rd, WC1 (242 0313), for their extensive range of emulsion and eggshell paints, hessian, felt and PVC.

Buck & Ryan
101 Tottenham Court Rd, W1 (636 7475) Warren St tube. Mon-Fri 8.30am-5.25, Sat 8.30am-1.00.
Tool merchants, woodworking hand tools, engraving, sculpting and metalwork. Also trade tools for carpentry, plumbing, building, engineering and the garden.

Candle Makers Supplies
28 Blythe Rd, W14 (602 1812) West Kensington tube. Mon-Sat 10.30am-6.00, closed Thu and between 1.00-2.00.
All supplies for candle makers. Batik wax, beginners' kits, beeswax and books on candlemaking.

L Cornelissen
22 Great Queen St, WC2 (405 3304) Holborn tube. Mon-Fri 9.30am-5.30, Sat 9.30am-4.30.
Beautiful old fashioned art shop, lined with pure pigment
146

in glass jars and antique wooden storage drawers. Paints, brushes, lithography and etching equipment.

Ehrman
21/22 Vicarage Gate, W8 (937 4568) Notting Hill Gate tube. Mon-Sat 10.00am-6.00.
Specialist tapestry shop, kits by Glorafilia, Needle Art, Metropolitan Museum of Art and the brilliant eclectic designs of Kaffe Fassett.

Falkiner Fine Papers
117 Long Acre, WC2 (240 2339) Covent Garden tube. Mon-Sat 10.00am-5.30.
Specialist papers. Especially for hand-made, marbled, Japanese, bookbinding and calligraphy.

Glorafilia
The Old Mill House, The Ridgeway, Mill Hill Village, NW7 (906 0212) Mill Hill East tube
Mon-Fri 10.00am-5.00, Sat 10.00am-12 noon.
Where the maestros of the innovative tapestry Jennifer Berman and Carol Lazurus sell their hand-painted kits for fireside evenings, especially those designs based upon the British Museum collections. Those less inclined to this domestic industry can find the hardware ready stitched — Victorian wicker and enamel workboxes, scissor cases, knitting bags, tapestry rolls amid Japanese and Victorian embroideries and wallhangings

Hobby Horse
15 Langton St, SW10 (351 1913) Sloane Sq tube, 11 and 22 bus.

Mon-Sat 10.00am-5.30.
Craft equipment for macrame, batik, basketry, weaving and beadwork.

Reeves
178 Kensington High St, W8 (937 5370) Kensington High St tube.
Mon-Fri 9.00am-5.30, Sat 9.00am-5.00.
Upstairs general artists' supplies, smocks, easels etc; downstairs for crafts, looms, enamelling, batik wax, dyes and raffia.

Seagull Model
15 Exhibition Rd, SW7 (584 2758) South Kensington tube.
Tue-Sat 10.30am-5.30.
Seagull are specialists in paper sculptures of a representational kind (as opposed to origami) 2D into 3D is a painstaking process but has great compulsive charm. Patients should try the skull (skeletons by order) paper birds, Lutyens castles and sailing ships.

Winsor and Newton
51 Rathbone Place, W1 (636 4231) Oxford Circus tube.
Mon-Sat 9.00am-5.30.
Large source of art supplies for the amateur and professional artist — canvas, sketchbooks, portfolios, all paints including glass paints and paints for children, Letraset, boxes and inks.

Yarncraft
112a Westbourne Grove, W2 (229 1432) Notting Hill Gate tube.
Mon-Sat 10.00am-5.00.
Specialists in handweaving yarns, wool, linen, cotton and silk especially the pure natural undyed sort. Plus dye kits, knitting wools, books on textile crafts, spinning and weaving equipment and classes for the needle crazy, lace to macrame.

Other general art supplies can be found at the following:
Chelsea Art Stores
314 King's Rd, SW3 (352 0430)
Wheatsheaf
76 Neal St, WC2 (836 7186)
Times Drawing Office
11/13 Pollen St, W1 (629 5661)
Rowney
12 Percy St, W1 (636 8241)
Graphic Art Centre
13 Tottenham St, W1 (637 2116)
*Good working stationery for office and home will be found at branches of **Rymans** all over London and a comprehensive range of their drawing office furniture at 18 High Holborn, WC1 (242 9819).*

Keith Johnson Photographic
Ramillies House, 1 Ramillies St, W1 (734 5641) Oxford Circus tube.
Mon-Fri 9.00am-5.30, Sat 9.30am-1.00.
The Camera House. One of the most comprehensive suppliers of photogoods for the professional and amateur. Equipment for rental and hire, chemicals, film printing materials.

Leeds Camera Centre
16 Brunswick St, WC1 (837 8039)

Russell Sq tube.
Mon-Fri 9.00am-5.00.
Specialists in second-hand camera equipment. Excellent range of all types of camera, plus lights, tripods, film stock. Helpful service and advice.

Techno Cameras
326 Euston Rd, NW1 (388 2871) Warren St/Great Portland St tube.
Mon-Fri 9.00am-5.30, Sat 9.00am-5.00.
Specialist in the SLR stocking every major brand. All lenses, accessories, film and chemicals. Also at 358 Kensington High St, W8; 120 Moorgate, EC2.

MUSIC

Early Music Shop
47 Chiltern St, W1 (935 1242) Bond St tube.
Mon-Fri 10.00am-5.30, Sat 10.00am-12.30, 1.30-4.00.
Pre-1800 reproduction instruments, predominantly keyboard. Kits and advice.

Paxman's
Langley St, WC2 (240 3647) Covent Garden tube.
Mon-Fri 9.00am-5.30, Sat 9.00am-12.30.
Where to blow your horn.

Salvi's
55 Endell St, WC2 (836 0788) Covent Garden tube.
Mon-Sat 10.00am-4.00.
Harps and all their strings.

RECORDS

Different branches of the

Oxford Street music centres, HMV and Virgin Records are sprinkled over London. Alternative stores include Our Price and Raven Records.

Collector's Corner
62 New Oxford St, W1 (580 6155) Tottenham Court Rd tube.
Mon-Fri 10.00am-6.00, Sat 10.00am-1.00
Obscure recordings, especially opera. Second-hand section.

FOLK JAZZ & BLUES

Dobells
21 Tower St, WC2 (2401 394) Covent Garden tube.
Mon-Sat 10.00am-7.00 (Jazz); Mon-Sat 10.00am-6.00 (Folk).
The best of all three.

James Asman
23a New Row, WC2 (240 1380) Leicester Sq tube.
Mon-Sat 10.00am-6.00
Old and new jazz.

R.&B. ROCK`N`ROLL

Vintage Record Centre
91 Roman Way, N7 (607 8586) King's Cross tube.
Mon-Fri 10.00am-5.00, Sat 10.00am-5.30
Vintage and second-hand. Also stock blues.

NOSTALGIA

That's Entertainment
43 The Market, Covent Garden, WC2 (240 2227) Covent Garden tube.

AUCTION HOUSES

Mon-Sat 10.00am-7.00
Rare, deleted and current kitsch. Especially soundtracks and musicals.

INDEPENDENTS

Rough Trade
202 Kensington Park Rd, W11
(229 8541)
Mon-Sat 10.30am-6.30
Flies the independent label. Singles, imports — blues to the newest wave.

THEATRICAL

Charles H Fox
22 Tavistock St, WC2 (240
3111) Covent Garden tube.
Mon-Fri 9.30am-5.00 closed
1.00-2.00
Charles Fox once staged the best theatrical costume sale in the city which ran and ran until they moved to the above address. Now for an excellent source of professional make up. Eyelure to Kensington Gore and for specialised costume hire (get your Santa rags here), plus swords and replica Crown Jewels from their subsidiary company Robert White & Sons.

Brodie & Middleton
68 Drury Lane, WC2 (836 3289)
Adlwych/Charing Cross tube.
Mon-Fri 8.30am-5.00
Theatrical suppliers for over 140 years — make up, pigments, powder colours, drapes etc for scenery, brushes and glitters.

AUCTION HOUSES

Sotheby Parke Bernet & Co
34/5 New Bond St, W1 (493
8080). Green Park tube.
Mon-Fri 9.30am-4.30
The oldest and grandest duke with huge turnover, over 500 sales of art and antiques a year. Investigate as a museum alternative, free and very civilised. Specialist sales of wine, vintage cars, textiles, armour and architectural drawings. Also at
Sotheby's Belgravia
19 Motcomb St, SW1 (235
4311). Knightsbridge tube.
Mon-Fri 9.30am-4.30
For Victoriana, Art Deco and Nouveau, collectables from 'La Belle Epoque' to Disneyland.

Christies
8 King St, SW1 (839 9060)
Green Park tube.
Mon 9.00am-7.00, Tue-Fri
9.00am-5.00
Important art and antiques found here with special sales of photography, toys, clocks and technical drawings. Less grand stuff at
Christies South Kensington
85 Old Brompton Rd, SW7
(581 2231) South Ken tube.
Mon-Fri 9.00am-5.00
Period costume, textiles, Art Deco and Nouveau, mechanical music, ephemera, cameras.

Phillips Son & Neale
Blenstock House, Blenheim St,
SW1 (629 6602). Bond St tube.
Mon-Fri 8.30am-5.00, Sat
8.30am-12.00 noon
The least awesome of the Big

Four. Strong and sharp on collectables: clocks, lead soldiers, postcards, books and studio ceramics as well as pictures and antiques. Also at

Phillips West

2 Salem Rd, W2 (221 5303)
Bayswater tube
Mon-Fri 9.00am-5.00 and Wed to 7.00, Sat 9.00am-12.00.
oak repro, Art Deco, and the antimacassar style.

Phillips Marylebone

Hayes Pl, Lisson Grove, NW1 (723 2647) Marylebone tube
Mon-Fri 9.00am-5.00, Sat 9.00am-12.00.
For the end of the Phillips line on Fridays. Junkier furniture with some but not many surprises.

Bonhams Montpelier Galleries

Montpelier St, SW7 (584 9161)
Knightsbridge tube.
Mon-Fri 9.00am-5.30
The smallest and dumpiest of the auction houses. Apart from the A & A, regular sales of fur, watercolours, ceramics, wine and scientific instruments. Also at
Bonhams Chelsea Galleries
65/89 Lots Rd, SW19 (352 0466). 11 or 22 bus
For the compulsive bric and bracs, weekly furniture on Tue, pictures, books and side effects fortnightly on Mon.

Stanley Gibbons Auctions

Drury House, Russell St. WC2 (836 8444). Covent Garden tube.
Mon-Fri 9.00am-5.30
Mainly stamps, but playing cards as a side line.

General Auctions

53/65 Garratt Lane, SW18 (870 3909) Wandsworth Town BR.
Viewing Fri 9.00am-12.30, sales Mon from 9.00am.
Apart from selling second-hand machines (typewriters to video), this is the best place to pick up a bike from the police's store; Edwardian rigid blacks or racers, whole or in pieces. Get there early.

Harvey's Auctions

22/23 Long Acre (240 1464)
Covent Garden tube.
Viewing Tue 9.30am-3.30, sales Wed from 10.30am
Comparatively new, bright spark for fair-priced antiques, furniture and decorative items.

Lots Road Galleries

71 Lots Rd, SW10 (352 2379) 11 and 22 bus.
Viewing Mon 9.00am-7.00, Tue 9.00am-6.00, sales Tue from 6.00
Furniture for a junk fiend's delight.

BOOKS

The London of the literary imagination will always seem greater than any grey monster that seethes and grinds about the modern pavements. Escape quick via the city's rich store of bookshops. The greats are **Foyles, Hatchards** *and the academic* **Dillons,** *chainstores include* **Claude Gill, Booksmith** *(for remainders) and* **WH Smith,** *though these can be limited for anything beyond best sellers, table glass and token Penguins.*

BOOKS

The streets of fame for specialist and second-hand books are Charing Cross Rd, Cecil Court, Covent Garden and Museum Street, though mad marketeers are bound to discover a finer bargain from the stalls of Portobello, especially for children's books.
If hard at heel why not join **Harrod's Lending Library** *Brompton Rd, SW1 (730 1234) especially for modern fiction or attempt membership to the exclusive book-lined rooms of the* **London Library** *14 St James Sq, SW1 (930 7705) whose Reading Room provides one of London's most civilised afternoons.*

ALTERNATIVE

The Alternative Bookshop
40 Floral St, WC2 (836 8371)
Covent Garden tube.
Mon-Sat 10.45am-6.00.
'Specialists in books on all aspects of individual liberty, the free market and the open society!' A bright anarchist bookstore waving the leaflet.

Atlantis Bookshop
49a Museum St, WC1 (405 2120) Tottenham Court Rd tube.
Mon-Fri 11.00am-5.30, Sat 11.00am-5.00.
New and second-hand books on the Occult and witchcraft, plus Tarot cards and crystal balls.

Colletts London Bookshop
64/66 Charing Cross Rd, WC2 (836 6306) Leicester Sq tube.
Mon-Wed 10.00am-6.30, Thu-

Fri 10.00am-7.00, Sat 10.00am-6.00.
Literature by, with and from the Left. Marxism, Fabianism, newspapers, badges with second-hand section.

Corner House Bookshop
14 Endell St, WC2 (836 7909)
Covent Garden tube.
Mon-Fri 10.00am-6.00, Sat 10.00am-7.00.
Radical education books, including feminist magazines, and non-sexist, non-racist children's books.

Forbidden Planet
23 Denmark St, WC2 (836 4179)
Mon-Sat 10.00am-6.00, Thu 10.00am-7.00.
Enormous science fiction stock. All the literature, comics, posters and non-fiction on the freaks, horrors and fantastic voyages of the cosmic imagination.

Kegan, Paul, Trench, Trubner Ltd
39 Store St, WC1 (636 1252)
Tottenham Court Rd tube.
Mon-Fri 9.00-5.30.
Specialists in Oriental and African studies. History, religion, politics etc with second-hand department.

Rudolf Steiner
38 Museum St, WC1 (242 4249)
Tottenham Court Rd tube.
Mon-Fri 10.00am-5.30.
Rudolf Steiner books by the shovelful. Buy the method religion and children's books.

Theosophical Book Shop
68 Russell St, WC1 (405 2309)

Tottenham Court Rd tube.
Mon-Sat 9.30-5.00.
*Get your instant Karma here.
All books religious and
esoteric: Tibetan Buddhism,
yoga, meditation, astrology,
Gurdjieff, Zen, Sufism, Taoism
and alternative medicine.*

Watkins Bookshop
21 Cecil Court, WC2 (836
3778) Leicester Sq tube.
Tue-Sat 10.00am-6.00.
*Specialists of the mystical and
exotic: alternative therapy,
oriental philosophy,
psychology, astrology,
meditation.*

ANTIQUARIAN

Bell, Book & Radmall
80 Long Acre, WC2 (240 2161)
Covent Garden tube.
Mon-Fri 10.00am-5.30.
*First edition bookshop,
especially modern fiction.*

Bertram Rota
30/31 Long Acre, WC2 (836
0723) Covent Garden tube.
Mon-Fri 9.30am-5.30.
*A glass-panelled bookshop
that dispels the myth that
antiquarian and second-hand
bookshops must be dark,
cluttered and mysterious to be
interesting. Do not be afraid of
the red-carpeted space, step in
and gather the first editions
here. Antiquarian, modern,
children's fiction, private
presses. The staff are amongst
the most helpful in London.*

Bondy
16 Little Russell St, WC1 (405
2733) Tottenham Court Rd
tube.

Erratic hours, ring first.
*Small dark shop specialising in
rare miniature books. Plus first
editions, early children's
books and histories of
caricature.*

Francis Edwards
83 Marylebone High St, W1
(953 9221) Baker St tube.
Mon-Fri 9.00am-5.00.
*Heavyweight bookshop,
established in 1855 and the
only one of its kind to be
custom built. The firm
specialise in early literature,
military and natural history
and autographed letters.
Expert advice and catalogues.*

Joseph
48a Charing Cross Rd, WC2
(836 4111) Leicester Sq tube.
Mon-Fri 9.00am-5.00.
*Antiquarian and second-hand
books especially for histories;
naval, military, natural and art,
and illustrated children's
books.*

Peter Eaton
80 Holland Park Ave, W11
(727 5211) Holland Park tube.
Mon-Sat 10.00am-5.00.
*Vast with glass and leather
spines. Upstairs for antiquarian
of general topics, downstairs
for a basement of second-hand
books.*

Maggs
50 Berkeley Sq, W1 (499 2051)
Bond St tube.
Mon-Fri 9.30am-5.00.
*Calm, carpeted, grand
booksellers. Private press
books, travel, early English
literature, manuscripts.
Catalogues and book
restoration service.*

BOOKS

Arthur Page
29 Museum St, WC1 (636 8206) Tottenham Court Rd tube.
Mon-Sat 10.30am-7.00, Sun 11.30am-7.00.
Literary second-hand and rare books, many music scores and biography. See also the bargain basement at 32 Coptic St, WC1.

Quaritch
5/8 Lower John St, Golden Sq, W1 (734 2983) Piccadilly Circus tube.
Mon-Fri 9.30am-5.30, closed for lunch 1.00-2.00.
The grand masters of literary dealing. Most of the stock is extremely old and rare and expensive. English literature, medicine, natural history, manuscripts, incunabula.

Sotherans
2-5 Sackville St, W1 (734 1150) Piccadilly Circus tube.
Mon-Fri 9.00am-5.30.
The oldest antiquarian booksellers, Sotherans are also famous for the purchase of Charles Dickens' library. Wide ranging stock including fine bindings, ornithology, rare books, autographs and old maps.

FOREIGN

Books From India
69 Great Russell St, WC1 (405 7226) Leicester Sq tube.
Mon-Fri 10.00am-5.30, Sat 10.00am-5.00.
Books in all the Indian languages, Indian travel books.

Collett's Chinese Gallery And Bookshop
40 Great Russell St, WC1 (580 7538) Tottenham Court Rd tube.
Mon-Sat 9.45am-5.45.
Where the little red book is surrounded by fluttering kites and silken embroideries. Books on Chinese art, medicine, the land, in Chinese and English, and dictionaries.

Collett's International Bookshop
129-131 Charing Cross Rd, WC2 (734 0782/3) Tottenham Court Rd tube.
Mon-Sat 9.30am-8.00.
The Russian bookshop. Books in and about Russian, text books Russian works in translation. Downstairs for the records and Polish posters.

Hachette Librarie Francaise
4 Regent Pl, W1 (734 5259) Piccadilly Circus tube.
Mon-Fri 9.30am-6.00, Sat 9.30am-1.00.
French bookshop for the Asterix-addicts and dictionary-clutching students ploughing their way through the Gallic superstars.

Orbis
66 Kenway St, SW5 (370 2210) South Kensington tube.
Mon-Fri 9.30am-5.30, Sat 9.30am-4.30.
All things Polish. Books on Poland and Eastern Europe in English and Polish, Polish books published in and outside Poland.

Paperbooks
28 Bute St, SW7 (584 2840) South Kensington tube.

Mon-Fri 10.00am-6.00, Sat
10.00am-5.00.
*French bookshop bright with
blue and white stripey awning,
strategically pres to the Lycee.
Mainlines in children's books,
French paperbacks and
elementary textbooks.
Cartoons by Claire Bretecher
on sale.*

Zeno
6 Denmark St, WC2 (836 2522)
Tottenham Court Rd, tube.
Mon-Fri 9.30am-6.00, Sat
10.00am-5.00.
*Classic and modern Greece.
Books on all aspects of Greece
and Cyprus:
travel, architecture and
literature, new, rare and
second-hand.*

J A Allen 1 Lower Grosvenor
Place, Buckingham Palace Rd,
SW1 (834 5606) Victoria tube.
Mon-Fri 9.00am-5.30, Sat
9.00am-1.00.
*The horseperson's bookshop.
Tomes on how to race, groom,
breed and ride the beasts.*

Arts Council Bookshop
8 Long Acre, WC2 (836 1359)
Leicester Sq tube.
Mon-Sat 10.00am-7.45.
*Lively rendering of books on
the performing arts and a fine
place to pick up the latest
cultural news, catalogues,
postcards, posters (especially
Polish) and poetry readings.*

Basilisk Press
32 England lane, NW3 (722
2142) Hampstead tube.
Mon-Sat 9.30am-5.30.

*Hand-made, private press and
limited edition books. Books
on bookmaking, slim poetic
volumes beautifully bound,
hand-marbled and hand-made
paper and original book
etchings.*

Cinema Bookshop
13 Great Russell St, WC1 (637
0206) Leicester Sq tube.
Thu-Sat 10.30am-5.30.
*Celluloid escapists hunt and
dream in technicolour. Books
about films from the silents to
the subtitled, on animation,
stars, televisions, posters and
stills.*

Costume And Fashion
Bookshop
Queen's Elm Parade, Old
Church St, SW3 (352 1176)
Sloane Sq tube.
Mon-Fri 9.30am-6.00, Sat
10.30am-1.00.
*Antiquarian and new books on
all aspects of costume, fashion,
textiles, embroidery and lace.*

Dance Books
9 Cecil Court, WC2 (836 2314)
Leicester Sq tube. Mon-Sat
11.00am-7.00.
*Photographs of this season's
heroes upon the wall. Dance
books on ballet, jazz, tap, folk,
ballroom etc, plus magazines
and American imports.*

Economist Bookshop
Clare Market, Portugal St,
WC2 (405 5531) Holborn tube.
Mon-Fri 9.30am-6.00, Wed
10.30am-6.00, Sat 10.00am-1.30
(LSE termtime only)
*Owned by The Economist and
the London School of
Economics, this bookshop is
heavy with the words of the*

BOOKS

social scientist. Get your statistics here. Next door for second-hand department.

Samuel French's Theatre Bookshop
14 Southampton St, WC2 (836 7513) Covent Garden tube.
Mon-Fri 9.30am-5.30.
Plays, theoretical and technical books on the theatre, sound effects, records and opera libretti.

London Art And Academy Bookshop
7/8 Holland St, W8 (937 6996) Kensington High St tube.
Mon-Sat 9.30am-6.00.
The London bookshop specialise in a vast range of architecture books; the Academy deviate into the popular arts, photography, illustration, crafts and design.

Modern Book Co
19/21 Praed St, W2 (402 9176) Edgware Rd tube.
Mon-Fri 9.00am-5.30, Sat 9.00am-1.00.
Technical bookshop. A siren away from the Gothic St Mary's Hospital. Not surprisingly, it stocks many medical books, plus engineering, electronics, law and accountancy.

Photographers Gallery
5 & 8 Great Newport St, WC2 (836 7860) Leicester Sq tube.
Mon-Sat 11.00am-7.00, Sun 12 noon-6.00.
Front of house shelves an excellent selection of books on and about photography and photographers. Catch the postcards.

Sims And Reed
5 Piccadilly Arcade, SW1 (493 0952) Piccadilly Circus tube.
Mon-Fri 10.00am-6.00.
Rare and antiquarian books, specialising in fine and applied arts amongst the windows of the Arcade.

Travel Bookshop
12 Abingdon Rd, W8 (938 1408) Kensington High St tube.
Tue-Fri 10.00am-6.00, Sat 10.00am-4.00.
Compulsive and imaginative bookstore for the explorer bored with Baedeker. Stock ranges from the greats of travel writing and old botanical, zoological, geographical and culinary guides with a special leaning towards Africa.

Zwemmer
76/80 Charing Cross Rd, WC2 (836 4710) Leicester Sq tube.
Mon-Fri 9.30am-5.30, Sat 9.30am-4.00.
Famous bookshop of the art world. Possibly the largest collection of art and architecture books in England, rare to remaindered.

CLOTHES

Most clothes shops are included in the area section but the following are either for those seeking a requirement other than sheer hedonistic delight - or situated in a part of London you wouldn't necesssarily roam for shops.

155

MEN'S CLOTHES

The English male is wary of fashion, taking it expensively in Bond Street, tailor cut in Savile Row, traditional in Jermyn Street and just cut in King's Road. There are some fairly gruesome chains strung along the main shopping highways but **Woodhouse** *with two branches in Oxford St, one in Kensington High St and Knightsbridge is a notable exception for* **Yves St Laurent, Cerruti,** *some leather, designer suits, classic knitwear and accessoires. Rich kids buy their leather from* **Loewe** *(Spanish) in Bond St, and* **Fendi** *(Italian, brilliantly dyed and furred), motorcyclists their racing form from* **Lewis Leathers** *120 Great Portland St, W1. The best second-hand places for men include* **Blax** *in Sicilian Ave* **Twentieth Century Box** *in Kings Rd, branches of* **Flip, Clozo** *in Islington Camden and Portobello Markets.*

Bates
21a Jermyn St, W1 (734 2722)
Piccadilly Circus tube.
Mon-Fri 9.00am-5.30, Sat
9.30am-12.30
Eccentric hatters in the old style — panamas, tweedies, boaters and felts.

Dash
15 Chiltern St, W1 (437 4383)
Baker St tube.
Mon-Sat 10.00am-6.00
Clever cut shop with jumpers, jackets, leather belts, cotton shirts etc selling for a third less than shops a mere stone's throw away. Riotous turnover, good style.

Deborah and Clare
14b Beauchamp Pl, SW3 (584 0641) Knightsbridge tube.
Mon-Fri 10.00am-6.00, Sat
10.00am-1.30
Ex-rock bespoke shirtmakers, cottons and silks.

Gieves & Hawkes
1 Saville Row, W1 (434 2001)
Oxford Circus tube.
Mon-Fri 9.00am-5.30, Sat
9.00am-1.00.
The naval and military flagship of Savile Row. Best for formal cuts.

Harvie & Hudson
77 Jermyn St, SW1 (930 3949)
and
Hilditch & Key
73 Jermyn St, SW1 (930 5336)
Piccadilly Circus tube.
Mon-Fri 9.00am-5.30, Sat
9.30am-4.30
Both are shirtmakers of old-fashioned kind — wooden drawers of wing collars, traditional ties, white pique, striped silks, engraved cufflinks and courteous service.

Module
49 South Molton St, W1 (493 3619) Bond St tube.
Mon-Sat 9.30am-6.00, Thu
10.00am-7.00
Youth and sportif, Continental stock, leather, classic striped shirts, thick jerseys.

Anthony Price
341 Kings Rd, SW3 (352 6893)
Sloane Sq tube.
Mon-Sat 10.30am-6.00
Bryan Ferry's tailor with a cold

CLOTHES

blue facade and surreal dummy behind glass. Classic hard-edge design. Choose the style from line drawing and colour swatches and don't forget the chequebook.

The Regal
Newburgh St, W1 ()
Oxford Circus tube.
Mon-Sat 10.00am-6.00
If you're still on that painting the town in flowers trip, you'll love this shop. Psychedelic clothing — velvet, hipster, Beatles caps, Dr K shirts, belts and florals.

Fillirossetti
177 New Bond St, W1 (491 7066) Bond St tube.
Mon-Sat 9.30am-5.30, Sat 9.30am-5.00
Traditional Italian shoes in unexpected colours — lilac to bronze. Unpretentious (a rare thing in this label-waving street) and excellent service.

Trickers
67 Jermyn St, SW1 (930 6395)
Piccadilly Circus tube.
Mon-Fri 9.00am-5.00, Sat 9.00am-12noon.
Traditional English shoes, brogues, oxfords, much shiny black and tan leather, all fashioned on the bench. Trickers sell their shoes to shops such as Browns and Crolla.

WOMEN'S CLOTHES

The famous streets of fashion are Bond Street and Knightsbridge. Keep away from these unless chequebook-happy or just looking. Oxford Street is for the chains, King's Road for the zap and tat, South Molton Street for the dashing designer's label, plus interesting pockets in Fulham Road (sheepskin addicts go to Janet Ibbotson in Pond Place), and Kensington. Probably the most dynamic and sharp-eyed of the chain fashion stores is Miss Selfridges who also star other labels such as Strawberry Studio and are strong on accessories. Otherwise take utility and silks from Warehouse, French Connection cotton and witty jumpers from Friends, oriental colour and glitter from Monsoon, flannel and jewel-bright knits from Benetton. Rummage for second hand at the end of Portobello Market, Camden Passage, Camden Lock, Kensington Market (for shops see index). For shoes look to the blossoming branches of Hobbs, Berties, Sacha, Rider, Accessoire in St Christopher's Pl, Walkers in Long Acre, Covent Garden. Classic feet walk to Rayne for royal leather and Charles Jourdan, in Knightsbridge especially for narrow fittings. The streets are Bond Street and South Molton St; cheapies are rife in Oxford St.

David Fielden
Antequarius, King's Rd, SW3 (351 1745) Sloane Sq tube.
Mon-Sat 10.30am-6.00
Specialist in wedding dresses made from antique lace, overflowing with detail, georgette taffeta and crepe de chine.

157

CLOTHES

The Dressing Room
81 George St, W1 (935 4772)
Baker St tube.
Mon-Sat 10.00am-7.00
*Runs as a fashion gallery
exhibiting the masters of old
British design. All clothes can
be made to order. Fashion
consultant and make-up artist
will iron out the problems.*

Long Tall Sally
40 Chiltern St, W1 (487 3370)
Bond St tube.
Mon-Fri 10.00am-6.00, Thu
10.00am-7.00, Sat 10.00am-4.00
*Specialises in clothes for the
extremely vertical. Classic safe
cuts.*

Nellie Frock
41 Chiltern St, W1 (486 2712)
Bond St tube.
Mon-Fri 10.00am-6.00, Thu
10.00am-7.00, Sat
*Clothes for the tiny. Also try
Chantal, 50 South Molton St,
and **Rich Bitch,** 85
Marylebone High St, W1.*

Scotch House
2 Brompton Rd, SW1 (581
2151) Knightsbridge tube.
Mon, Tue, Thu 9.00am-5.30,
Wed 9.00am-6.30, Fri, Sat
9.00am-6.00
*Where the Highland tartan
rules. Scottish knitwear, Aran
and Fair Isle lambswool,
Shetland and cashmere.*

Laurence Corner
62 Hampstead Rd, NW1 (388
6811) Warren St tube.
Mon-Sat 9.00am-5.30
*There are small outfits of
Army Surplus throughout
London but none so large or
comprehensive as Laurence
Corner. Knockers of the
establishment would not feel
at ease within its walls. On the
whole the uniforms are of the
duller sort; khaki is
everywhere. In the second-
hand range there are flying
and boiler suits, sailors' serge,
naval jumpers, army
greatcoats, combat jackets.
One of the best places to
collect winter woollens (heavy
speckled socks, long johns)
and summer singlets.*

Damart
263 Regent St, W1 (629 2364)
Oxford Circus tube.
Mon-Fri 9.00am-5.30, Thu
9.00am-6.30, Sat 9.00am-5.00
*Palace of the thermal
underwear. Snigger until the
icy blasts beckon snow.*

PX
Endell St, WC2
Covent Garden tube
*Theatrical costume for the
street players. Much bizarre
velvet, taffeta, bright satin and
looking in the mirror.
Downstairs for nighttime's
mad hatter, Stephen Jones.*

CHILDRENS CLOTHES

Bambino
57 Golders Green Rd, NW11
(458 1541) Golders Green tube
Mon-Sat 9.00am-6.00.
*Mini-fashion in the right
colours. Sophisticated
babywear, excellent Italian
baby equipment, witty
swimwear, bright French and
Italian clothes for the in (but not
formal)-kids. Fish tanks,
blackboard and slides keep
them quiet while you look.*

CLOTHES

Laura Ashley
(Children's Shop) 75 Lower
Sloane St, SW1 (730 5255)
Sloane Sq tube.
Mon-Fri 9.30am-6.00, Sat
10.00am-5.30.
*Where to catch the lost
innocence style early. Peasant
cotton, flower-sprigged
dresses, velvet knickerbockers,
white blouses, Alice in
Wonderland white aprons,
straw hats, corduroy, plus
large bridesmaid and page
section.*

Little Horrors
16 Cheval Pl, SW1 (589
5289)Knightsbridge tube.
Mon-Fri 9.30am-6.00, Sat
10.00am-5.30.
*Large, expensive shop for
those who only cut French and
Italian. Extensive range of
Cacherel, Pierre Cardin
swimwear, silken party
dresses, fine wool pyjamas, all
leather sandals and Valentino
suits for tiny stockbrockers.*

Rowes
170 New Bond St, W1 (734
9711) Bond St tube.
Mon-Fri 9.00am-5.30, Sat
9.00am-5.00.
*One of the oldest children's
shops in London (Rowes were
the first to make sailor suits).
Traditional mixed with
Cacherel. Good for made to
measure baby wear and party
clothes, old fashioned shoes
and riding clothes.*

Welcome To The World
90 Golders Green Rd, NW11
(455 2261) Golders Green tube.
Mon-Sat 9.30am-5.00.
*Excellent nursery design
serivce, including re-dressing
cribs in imported American
fabrics, fresh gingham and
broderie anglaise. Four poster
cots, accessories, baby clothes,
teddy bears (including one that
simulates womb noises) and
gifts for the new-born
delivered to any London
hospital.*

SECOND HAND

Children's Bazaar
162 Sloane St, SW1 (730 8901)
Sloane Sq tube.
Mon-Fri 9.30am-5.00
*As might be expected from its
location, the Children's Bazaar
keeps a very straight cut of
cloth. Ideal for making them
look well-behaved are the
classic tweed coats, smocked
dresses boys' suits and patent
party shoes. Ages from 0-16.*

Outgroans
190 Albany St, NW1 (387 2018)
Camden Town tube.
Tue-Fri 10.00am-5.00, Sat
10.00am-1.00
*Wide variety of children's
clothes (except for shoes and
underwear)... anoraks,
babywear, end of lines (eg Jean
Le Bourge towelling kits from
Meals). Outgroans sell
customers' clothes keeping
them for two months and
giving 50% of the selling price
(go on Tuesdays, Wednesday
and Thursdays)*

Second to None
10 Bassett Rd, W19 (969 5872)
Ladbroke Grove.
Tue only 10.00am-4.30
*Set in the basement of a
whitefaced house, Second to
None is an excellent find*

Amazingly cheap (some at a fifth of the price). Harris tweed coats with velvet collars for erstwhile Christopher Robins. Others snap up Liberty print dresses, knickerbockers of tough cord, and thick knit jumpers and a huge box of dungarees. The shoe section includes gumboots, sandals, ballet shoes, ice-skating boots, moon boots and there are also cots, prams and all the hardware a baby could wish for.

Small Change
25 Carnegie House, New End, NW3 (794 3043)
Tue-Fri 10.00am-4.30, Sat 10.00am-1.00
Good selection of the less formal, including snow suits, riding clothes, belts, leotards and tap shoes. Small Change will also sell customers' clothes on the same basis as Outgroans.

HOME

Aram Designs
3 Kean St, WC2 (240 3933)
Holborn tube.
Mon-Fri 9.30am-5.30.
Modern pioneer furniture of the sleek Italian kind. More for those interested in design than practicality. Includes the Eileen Gray collection.

Co-Existence
2 Conduit Buildings, Floral St, WC2 (240 2746) Covent Garden tube.
Mon-Fri 10.00am-6.00, Sat 11.00am-6.00.
Ancient and modern mix, furniture of the large cold Continental kind, futurist lighting, fabrics, wallpapers etc. Interior decoration services include upholstery framing, garden planning.

The Colefax and Fowler Chintz Shop
149 Ebury St, SW1 (730 2173)
Victoria tube.
Mon-Fri 9.30am-1.00, 2.00-5.30.
Home of the leafy English chintz. Cut from the original pattern books of the 18th and 19th centuries.

Futon Company
267 Archway Rd, N7 (340 6126)
Highgate tube.
Tue-Sat 10.30am-6.00.
Back to the floor sleepers roll their bed and walk here.

Chisholm's
103 Kingsway, WC2 (405 0992)
Holborn tube.
Mon-Fri 9.00am-5.30.
Stationery and office supplies but famous for stocking Filofax, the moving filing cabinet. Paper fiends grab the essential loose leaves (over a hundred in design from tracing paper to blotting paper, ledgers, maps and carbons) and encased in strong pocketed leather.

Coles
18 Mortimer St, W1 (580 1066)
Oxford Circus tube.
Mon-Fri 10.00am-5.00.
Hand blocked wallpapers, hessian and own dynamic range of coloured paints and emulsions. Will make to customer specifications and colour schemes. Good for historical print and french wallpapers.

HOME

Cooker Centre
420 Edgware Rd, W2 (723
2975) Edgware Rd tube.
Mon-Fri 8.30am-5.30, Thu
8.30am-1.00, Sat 8.30am-4.30.
*Discount and second-hand gas
cookers, plus part exchange.*

The Dried Flower Shop
67 Highbury Park, N5 (354
2976) Canonbury tube
Tue-Sat 10.00am-5.30.
*Vast array of dried flowers
from wild Australians to
cultivated English with or
without arrangement.*

Felt and Hessian Shop
34 Greville St, EC1 (405 6215)
Farringdon tube
Mon-Fri 9.00am-5.00.
*Coloured felts, backed and
unbacked hessians in
boundless metre.*

Homeworks
Dove Lane, 107 Pimlico Rd,
SW2 (730 9116) Sloane Sq
tube.
Mon-Fri 9.30am-5.30.
*Robin Guild's once-warehouse,
now gallery of ideas for the
designer. Dynamic mix of
modern and antique, Eastern
carpet to space kitchen.*

SKK Lighting
41a Belsize Lane, NW3 (431
0451) Swiss Cottage tube
Ring for appointment.
*Where the whizz-kid of modern
lighting Shiu Kay Kan has his
workshop. Giacometti-thin
metal day-glo parachute, nylon
crumpled or taut as a kite,
anodized tin shade.*
Find also at:
Mr Light, *Fulham and King's
Rd, SW3.*

Sutton Seeds
33 Catherine St, WC2 (836
0619) Covent Garden tube.
Mon-Fri 9.30am-5.30.
*Sutton's seed store, plus
fertilizers, insecticides and
gardening advice.*

Syon Park Nursery
Syon Park, Brentford,
Middlesex (568 0134)
Brentford BR
Mon-Sat 9.30am-4.45, Sun
10.00am-4.45.
*Apart from serving as perfect
excuse to walk on the green-
spaced glory of the park and
visit the extra-ordinary
Butterfly House, this is an
excellent gardening centre.*

Townsends
1 Church St, NW8 (724 3746)
Edgware Rd tube.
Tue-Sat 10.15am-6.00.
*The tile place, old, blue and
white, figurative, plus
fireplaces, glazed doors and
stained glass.*

The Bedchamber
3 Cadogan St, SW3 (589 1860)
South Kensington tube.
Mon-Fri 9.30am-5.30, Sat
9.30am-1.00.
*Where to catch the zzz's in the
grand, old style. Antique and
reproduction four-poster beds,
brass and wood, and quilts to
brighten them. Made to order.*

The London Stove Centre
49 Chiltern St, W1 (486 5168)
Bond St tube.
Tue-Sat 10.0am-6.00, Thu
10.00am-7.00.
*Those into solid heat fetch the
stove here. Modern English,
American and European
stoves and cookers, pipes and*

hods in economic gleaming. Plus specialist flue service, advice on chimney sweeps, where to order smokeless fuels etc.

The Space Saving Bed Centre
13/14 Golden Sq, W1 (734 4246) Piccadilly Circus tube Mon-Sat 9.00am-5.30, Wed 9.00am-4.30, Thu 9.00am-7.00. *Interlock, changeabout, fit in, break up, spread out, hide away...you can do lots of things with a bed. Here they turn into sofas, tables, seats, singles and doubles or disappear into the wall, a cupboard or stack beneath one another. Function before beauty.*

SERVICES

BADGES
The Badge Shop
49 Earlham St, WC2 (836 9327).

BATHS
Renubath
596 Chiswick High Rd, W4 (995 5252)

BEDS
The London Bedding Centre
26/27 Sloane St, SW1 (235 7542).

BIKES
(see sports)

BOOKS
Sangorski & Sutcliffe
1 Poland St, W1 (437 2252)
Resew and hand bind.

BLINDS
Daylight Studio
119 Regent's Park Rd, NW1 (586 3911)
Hand-paint roller blinds and chair canvas. Also murals.

Blind Alley
Camden Lock, Commercial Place, NW1 (485 8030)
Roller blind commissions. Venetian blinds to order at branches of **Habitat** *and* **John Lewis.**

CAKES
House of Floris
39 Brewer St, W1 (437 5755).

Maison Bertaux
28 Greek St, W1 (437 6007).

Maison Bouquillon
41/45 Moscow Rd, W2 (727 4897); 28 Westbourne Grove, W2 (229 2107).

Maison Pechon
127 Queensway, W2 (229 0746).

CARPETS
David Black
96 Portland Rd, W11 (727 2566)

CHILDREN'S CLOTHES
Rowes
170 New Bond St, W1 (734 9711).
Expensive tailory.

Sally Membury
1 Church Rd, Barnes, SW13
Made to order. Smocks to party dresses. (876 2910)

CHINA
Chinamend
54 Walton St, SW1 (589 1182)
Cures the crash.

CHOCOLATES
Charbonnel & Walker

28 Old Bond St, W1 (629 4396/5149)
Boites blanches, boxes with chocolate messages.

Prestat
24 South Molton St, W1 (629 4838).
Chocolate commissions and telegrams.

CLEANERS
There are Sketchleys and their ilk on every corner. Specialised services, need the main branch of
Jeeves
8 & 10 Pont Street, SW1 (235 1101) *for dry cleaning, repairs and alterations; No 9 for the laundering of fine shirts and linen; No 7 for cobbling. Plus fur and leather restoration, curtain hanging and holiday packaging.*

COPPER
The Copper Shop
48 Neal St, WC2 (836 2984)
Retinning.

DOLLS
The Doll's Hospital
16 Dawes Rd, SW6 (385 2081)
Broken old dolls and teddy bears who have seen better times.

DYERS
Chalfont Cleaners & Dyers
222 Baker St, W1 (935 7316)

FRAMING
Blackman Harvey
29 Earlham St, WC2 (836 1904).

Rowley
115 Kensington Church St, W8 (727 6495).

Evans the Frame
71 Regent's Park Rd, NW1 (722 2009).

FURNITURE
The Shop For Painted Furniture
94 Waterford Rd, SW6 (736 1908)
General.

Sitting Pretty
131 Dawes Rd, SW6 (381 0049)
Loos.

Dragons
25 Walton St, SW1 (589 3795)
Children.

Hippo Hall
65 Pimlico Rd, SW1 (730 7710)
Children. Also murals.

HATS
David Shilling
36 Marylebone High St, W1 (487 3179)
The grand and zany for women.

George Malyard
137 Lavender Hill, SW11 (223 8292)
Men's traditional.

JEWELLERY
G Garbe
23 Charlotte St, W1 (636 1268)
Plus jade and fans.

KNIVES
Divertimenti
68/72 Marylebone Lane, W1 (935 0689)
Sharpening.

LAMPS

Clare House
35 Elizabeth St, SW1 (730 8484)

*Will convert almost anything
into a lighting fixture.*

PAINT
John Oliver
33 Pembridge Rd, W11 (727
3735)
Mix to order.

PENS
Pencraft
119 Regent St, W1 (734 4928)

POSTERS
The Poster Shop
1 Chalk Farm Rd, NW1 (267 6985)

The Vintage Magazine Store
Brewer St, W1 (438 8525).

SHIRTS
Turnbull & Asser
71/72 Jermyn St, SW1 (930
0502)
*One of the several bespoke
shirtmakers in this well-
tailored street.*

SHOES
Lobb's
9 St James St, SW1 (930 3664)
See also
Trickers
in Jermyn St and
Anthony Lloyd-Jennings
in New Bond St.
(Clogs)

Gohil's
246 Camden High St, NW1
(485 9195)
(Eccentric)

Andy's
61 Goldhawk Rd, W12 (743
4978)

The Little Shoe Box
89 Holloway Rd, N7 (607 1247).
(Orthopaedic)

James Taylor & Son
4 Paddington St, W1 (935 4149)
Plus bespoke.

SOFT SCULPTURE
Stuffed
23 Beak St, W1 (437 7311)

STATIONERY
Smythson
54 New Bond St, W1 (629
8558)
*Plus visiting cards, sealing
wax and menus.*

**The Walton Street Stationery
Co**
97 Walton St, SW3 (589 0777).

WALLPAPER
Coles
18 Mortimer St, W1 (580 1066)
*Commission your own wall or
colour.*

SPORT SHOPS

Lillywhites Piccadilly Circus,
SW1 (284 3162) Piccadilly
Circus tube. Mon-Sat
9.00am-6.00, Thu 9.00am-7.00,
and **Harrods Olympic Way**
4th Floor, Brompton Rd, SW1
(730 1234) Mon-Sat
9.00am-6.00, Wed 9.00am-7.00,
*are for the undecided and
those who aren't dynamically
interested in the difference
between Slazenger and Stuart
Surridge. Both cover most
ranges of recreational and
outdoor sports with a rather
stronger emphasis on fashion
and social whim than
specialist equipment,
adapting their stock to
seasonal demands (ie skiing
in winter, tennis in summer)
Service and merchandise can*

be frustrating for the serious sportsperson. The smaller shops listed below are run by actual sportsmen who concentrate in a specific field and can give advice. There are many High St sports shops but a trip to the specialist is worth the marathon effort.

ARCHERY

The Archery Centre
290 High St, Croydon, Middlesex (686 1686) East & West Croydon BR.
Mon-Fri 9.00am-5.30, Sat 9.00am-5.00, closed Wed.
The only real archery shop in London. Huge range of equipment from the beginnerr to the world champion. For practice space write to Grand National Archery Society, National Agricultural Centre, Stoneleigh, Kenilworth, Warwicks (0203 23907)

BILLIARDS & SNOOKER

Thurston and Co
200 Camden High St, NW1 (267 5367) Camden Town tube.
Mon-Sat 8.30-5.30.
Thurston's factory was first established in 1799 and have ever since been world famous for their green baize tables. Traditional and modern tables, Standfast models, made to order and accessories in newish showroom.

BOARD GAMES

The Chess Centre
3 Harcourt St, W1 (402 5393)

Edgware Rd tube. Mon-Fri 9.30am-5.30, Sat 9.30am-4.00.
Over 100 different types of chess sets from tiny travel sets to the hand-sculpted antique. Computer chess, score sheets, clocks, ties and chess lit.

The Games Centre
22 Oxford St, W1 (637 7911) Tottenham Court Rd tube.
Mon-Sat 9.30am-10.00.
Largest and widest selection of indoor games in London. Specialist department in role-playing SF games, fantasy and war games. Electronic games, card tables, casino equipment, jigsaw puzzles and translated games, eg Arabic monopoly and Russian scrabble. Also at 439 Oxford St, W1; 126 Charing Cross Rd, WC1; 184 Regent St, W1.

Just Games
62 Brewer St, W1 (437 0761) Piccadilly Circus tube. Mon-Sat 10.00am-6.00, Thu 10.00am-7.00.
Smaller indoor games shop with a large selection of playing cards and executive toys.

Village Games
15 Kingswell, Heath St, NW3 (435 3101) Hampstead Heath tube. Mon-Sat 10.00am-6.00.
Northern space for the board fiends. Fantasy games and twenty different sorts of tarot cards.

BIKES

Alans Cycles
79a Wandsworth Rd, SW8 (622 9077) Clapham South tube.

Mon-Sat 9.15am-6.15.
One of the few places to part exchange. Stocks traditional range of bikes, repairs and key-cutting service.

Beta Bikes
275 West End Lane, NW6 (794 4133) West Hampstead tube. Mon-Sat 9.00am-6.00, Sun 11.00am-1.00, closed Thu.
Touring, racing and children's bikes. Some tandems.

Bell St Bikes
73 Bell St, NW1 (724 0456) Edgware Rd tube. Mon-Sat 10.00am-6.00, closed Thu.
New and second-hand bikes for children and adults. Accessories, repairs and hire service.

EJ Barnes
285 Westbourne Grove, W11 (727 5147) Notting Hill Gate/Ladbroke Grove tube. Mon-Sat 11.00am-7.00.
Good range of manufacturers, eg Claude Butler, Carlton and Raleigh. Second-hand, part-exchange, children's, long time repair man of the 'Portobello pushbike people'.

Covent Garden Cycles
41 Shorts Gardens, WC2 (836 1752) Covent Garden tube, Mon-Fri 10.00am-9.00, Wed 10.00am-2.00, Sat 10.00am-6.00.
Specialists in French cycles with a fine selection of sleek Peugeot frames. Touring and commuter bikes, some second-hand, repairs (priority for those bought at the shop)

Tandem Centre
281 Old Kent Rd, SE1 (231 1641) Elephant & Castle tube,

then bus. Mon-Sat 9.00am-6.00.
Designers and sellers of their own tandems, the Globetrotter range from touring to fierce competition. Will make to order and repairs. Extremely friendly and helpful.

The Victoria Cycling Co
53/55 Pimlico Rd, SW1 (730 6898) Sloane Sq tube. Mon-Sat 9.00am-6.00.
Very efficient bike store with a full range of conventional models for children and adults. Spare parts service, in-house insurance scheme, accessories.

FISHING

Farlow's
5 Pall Mall, SW1 (839 2423) Piccadilly Circus tube. Mon-Fri 9.00am-5.00, Sat 9.00am-12 noon.
Established in 1840, this fine all round angling shop caters for the angler of sea, loch, course, game and fly. Carbon fibre rods, wet and dry flies, rod repairs and defensive clothing.

House of Hardy
61 Pall Mall, SW1 (839 5515) Green Park tube. Mon-Fri 9.00am-5.00.
Gentleman's fishing house with a royal nod of approval and an inevitable lean towards the king salmon. Brilliantly equipped, not for the searcher of Serpentine stickleback.

RIDING

The Huntsman
11 Savile Row, W1 (734 7441)

Oxford Circus. Mon-Fri
9.00am-5.45, closed for lunch
1.00-2.00.
*Specialists in the hand-made
hunting habit, jacket and
jodhpurs. Boots downstairs.*

Moss Bros
Bedford St, WC2 (240 4567)
Leicester Sq tube. Mon-Sat
9.00am-5.00, Thu 9.00am-7.00.
*Gallant and generally
successful attempt to provide
for every equestrian sport. Tack
and clothes (plus very chic
breeches) for racing, eventing,
polo and muddy hack.*

George Parkes
12 Upper St Martins Lane,
WC2 (836 1164) Leicester Sq
tube. Mon-Fri 9.00am-5.00.
*Delicious smell of new
creaking leather. Saddles and
polo equipment, especially the
sticks.*

RUNNING

Cobra Sports
48 Long Acre, WC2 (835 0805)
Covent Garden tube. Mon-Sat
9.30am-7.30.
*Bright sports-jazz shoes for the
main track. This branch of
specialist sports shoe shops
have expanded over the last
two and a half years with the
healthy jogging hordes and
marathon madness. Training
shoes (especially Nike and
Znew Balance) spikes,
basketball, rugby, soccer, and
tennis footwear and imported
American running gear. Also
at 394 King's Rd, SW10; 35 The
Quadrant, Richmond, Middx;
110 Westbourne Grove, W2.*

SKATING

Queens' Ice Rink Shop
Queensway, W2 (229 4859)
Queensway tube. Mon-Sun
10.00am-12 noon, 2.00-5.00,
7.00-10.00.
*Miniest skating skirts for the
middle-rink dazzlers, sensible
gloves for those who fall over,
new and second-hand boots.
The rink is open at the same
times (weekend evenings
being the most expensive)
private sessions, children's
classes (for rollerskating see
Alpine Sports)*

SKI-ING

Alpine Sports
10/12 Holborn, WC1 (404
5681) Holborn tube. Mon-Sat
10.00am-6.00, Thu 10.00am-7.00.
*Less grand piste artistes. With
sections for cross country
skiing and mountaineering
plus overhaul and repair
services. Summer finds the
action in windsurfing,
rollerskating, tennis, racket
sports, BXM, skateboards,
surfing.*

Sun & Snow
299 Brompton Rd, SW1 (581
2039) South Kensington tube.
Mon-Sat 9.30am-6.00, Wed
9.30am-7.00.
*Ski equipment and clothing for
the stylish schuss. Workshop
facilities.*

TENNIS

The Racket Shop
22 Northland Rd, W11 (603 0013)

Goldhawk Rd, tube.
Mon-Sat 10.00am-6.00, Thu
10.00am-1.00.
*International range of rackets
including Dunlop, Donnay,
Price and Slazenger. Best
known for quality stringing
and repair service.*

Sports Drobny
33 Thurloe Place, SW7 (581
2934) South Kensington tube.
Mon-Fri 10.00am-5.30, Sat
9.30am-1.00.
*Unpretentious general sports
shop with direct speciality in
tennis. String and racquet
repairs done by one of the few
Englishmen to win
Wimbledon.*

WATER SPORTS

Thames Water Sports
479 Fulham Palace Rd, SW6
(381 0558) Fulham Broadway.
Mon-Sat 9.00am-6.00.
*Take it under with Thames
specialist diving equipment,
beginners to professionals —
wet suits, cylinders, knives,
masks, flippers, underwater
cameras. For information
about training write to:*
Sub Acqua Association
34 Buckingham Palace Rd,
SU1 (828 4551);

British Sub-Acqua Club
70 Brompton Rd, SW3 (387
9302)

BOATS

*In spite of the wide and
lapping Thames, London is
not the best place to buy
boats, except for the post
Christmas Boat Show held at
Earls Court Exhibtion Centre.
But if stuck in the city try:*
Inflatable Boat Centre
227 Brighton Rd, South
Croydon, Surrey (688 3431) for
inflatables;

Proctor
15 Este Rd, SW11 (288 5911)
for racing sailboats, chandlery
and sailing wear;

Tony Williams
Northwood Boating Centre,
Station Approach, Northwood,
Middx (Northwood 23231) for
power boats;

London Dinghy Centre
54a Carter Lane, EC4 (248
6303) for dinghies;

Boat Showrooms of London
286 Kensington High St, W8
(602 0123) for yachts.

WHERE TO GO

*Outdoor sports throughout
the Metropolitan area are
provided by the GLC for a
minimal charge though do
not often extend beyond
muddy football pitches and
decaying hard tennis courts
(Clapham Common has
floodlit courts Mon-Wed) Ring
Parks Dept GLC County Hall,
SE1 (633 5000) and Facilities
Division, The Sports Council,*

SPORTS CENTRES

160 Great Portland St, W1 (358 1277) for information.

SPORTS CENTRES

All the centres listed below are open seven days a week and have facilities for squash, tennis, basketball, 5-a-side football, table tennis, badmington, handball, netball and fives

Crystal Palace National Sports Centre
Ledrington Rd, Norwood, SE19 (778 0131) Crystal Palace BR.
Three pools plus all standard sports, including regular afternoon courses in Swimming, karate, tennis, athletics and squash.

Finsbury Leisure Centre
Norman St, EC1 (253 4490) Old St tube.
Roller skating/disco, gymnastics, judo, trampolining, children's activities, archery.

Michael Sobell Sports Centre
Hornsey Rd, N7 (607 1632) Finsbury Park tube.
Indoor ski slope, ice skating, judo, children's programmes throughout holidays.

Jubliee Recreation Centre
Central Market, Covent Garden, WC2 (836 2799) Covent Garden tube.
Trampolining, roller skating.

DANCE

Dance Centre
20 Floral St, WC2 (379 3303)
Covent Garden tube. Mon-Fri 9.00am-8.00, Sat 9.00am-6.00.
White-tiled bright lit dance shop for energetic leotards, leg warmers, tracksuits in a myriad colours and dance shoes. Wide range of classes.

Pineapple Dance Centre
7 Langley St, WC2 (836 4004) Covent Garden tube. Mon-Fri 9.00am-9.00, Sat 10.00am-6.00, Sun 12 noon-5.00.
Nine studios for toe-tapping, jazz-beating, yoga-stretching, ballet-spinning-beginners to professional. Plus classic belly dancing, juggling, classes for kids and mime. Dance shop stocks the latest in dance wear, shuffle shoes and ballet accessories. Membership. Health bar and dance board.

RIDING STABLES

Bathurst Riding Stables
63 Bathurst Mews, W2 (723 2813)
Open everyday (no rides on Mon) Lancaster Gate tube

Roehampton Gate Riding and Livery Stables
Priory Lane, SW15 (876 7089) Putney Bridge tube
Open every day except Mon
Rides in Richmond Park, for those who want to escape the circular confines of Rotten Row.

Ross Nye
8 Bathurst Mews, W2 (262 3791) Lancaster Gate tube.
Open every day except Mon and Thu
Rides and tuition in Hyde Park.

SUNDAY CHECKLIST

ANTIQUES

Camden Lock Market
Commercial Place, NW1.
10.00am-5.30.
Clocks, bicycles, period clothes, curios.

BOOKS

NEW
The Pan Bookshop
158 Fulham Rd, SW3 (373 4997)
2.30-6.30.

OLD
Arthur Page
29 Museum St, WC1 (636 8206)
11.30am-7.00.

Piccadilly Rare Books
30 Sackville St, W1 (437 2135)

TOYS

Patricks
107/111 Lillie Rd, SW6 (385 9864)
9.00am-1.00.

CLOTHES

Dickie Dirts
58a Westbourne Grove, W2 (229 1466)
9.00am-11.00pm.
A quick pair of jeans, cheap shirts etc. Also at: North End Rd, Fulham Broadway, SW6; Victoria St, SW1.

Flip
96/98 Curtain Rd, EC2 (729 4341)
11.00am-3.30.
New and old Americana, the ubiquitous sweatshirt to a fifties party dress. Also at: 116 Long Acre, WC2 (836 9851) 11.00am-6.30.

Hotline
36/38 Westbourne Grove, W2 (221 7782)
12 noon-7.00.
Cheap and splash-bright clothes, especially for stripey T-shirts and shoes, Chinese sandals, pumps and baseball boots.

Kingsley
25 Chalk Farm Rd, NW1 (267 9403)
10.30am-5.00.
American and Italian clothes for men.
See also **Brick Lane** *and Petticoat Lane Markets, E1.* Mornings.

FOOD

On most corners are to be found one or two hard-working little stores which stay open during the unsociable hours. Fruit and veg can be found at the following markets:

East Street Market
Walworth Rd, SE17.
8.00am-1.00

Chapel Street Market
Islington, N1
The city's 24-hour Supermarket is in Westbourne Grove, W2.

CHINESE
The Great Wall
31-37 Wardour St, W1 (437 796
11.00am-8.00.

SUNDAY CHECKLIST

CHOCOLATES
Clare's Chocolates
3 Park Rd, NW1 (262 1906)
10.00am-5.00.

DELICATESSENS
Here is Food
26 The Pavement, Clapham
Common, SW4 (622 6818)
10.00am-9.00.

Mr Christians
11 Elgin Crescent, W11 (229
0501)
9.30am-2.00.

Olga Stores
30 Penton St, N1 (837 5467)
9.00am-1.00.

Partridges
132 Sloane St, SW1 (730 0651)
10.00am-8.00.

Richmond Hill Delicatessen
22 Richmond Hill, Richmond,
Surrey (940 3952)
10.00am-9.00.

FISH
Bob White
1 Kennington Lane, SE11 (785
1931)
10.00am-2.00
*Also a shellfish stall at the
Oval.*

HEALTH FOOD
Chalk Farm Nutrition Centre
41 Chalk Farm Rd, NW1 (485
0116)
10.00am-7.00.

Osaka
7 Goldhurst Terrace, NW6
(624 4983)
11.00am-7.00.

ICES
Marine Ices
8 Haverstock Hill, NW3 (485
8898)
11.00am-11.00.

PATISSERIES
Maison Bouquillon
41/45 Moscow Rd, W2 (727
4897) 8.00am-1.00;
28 Westbourne Grove, W2
(229 2107)
9.00am-11.00pm.

Maison Bertraux
28 Greek St, W1 (437 6007)
9.30am-1.00.

REAL ALE
The Grog Blossom
253 West End Lane, NW6 (794
7808)
Open till 10.00.

HOME

BIKES/HIRE AND SELL
Dial-A-Bike
2 Denbigh Mews, SW1 (834
0756)

London Bicycle Company
41, Floral St, WC2 (836 7830)
Mon-Sat 9.00am-6.00.

CHEMISTS
Boots
Piccadilly Circus, W1 (930
4761)
24 hour.

Bliss
54 Willesden Lane, NW6 (624
8000)
24 hour.

Warman Freed
45 Golders Green Rd, NW11
(455 4351)
10.00am-12.00 midnight.

John Bell and Croyden
54 Wigmore St, W1 (935 5555)
10.00am-8.00.

Underwoods
75 Queensway, W2 (229 9266)
10.00am-10.00.

CHINA
Reject China Shop
33-35 Beauchamp Place, SW3
(584 9409)
10.00am-5.00.

GARDEN
Clifton Nurseries
5a Clifton Villas, W9 (286 9888)
10.30am-1.00.

GENERAL
Columbia St Market
Bethnal Green Rd, E1.
9.00am-1.00.

FURNITURE
*The area to go to on Sunday is
Camden where all the shops
about the Lock Market are
open to lure the crowds: take
away old stoves at the* **Stove
Shop,** *blinds at* **Blind Alley,**
the best crafts at the **Lock
Shop,** *terracotta and tiles at*
Casa Catalan *and food from
the several rich delicatessens.
See also* **Covent Garden Market**

Houndsditch Warehouse
Houndsditch EC3 (283 3131)
9.30am-2.00.

The Pine Shop
176/178 West End Lane, NW6
(435 0144)
10.00am-1.00.

MOTOR SPARES
Autoplus
198 West End Lane, NW6 (435
1727)
10.00am-2.00.

Lively Motors
25-29 Fulham High St, SW6
(736 4763)
9.30am-12.30.

Latchmere Motor Spares
95 Latchmere Rd, SW4 (228
3901).

NEWSPAPERS
Moroni & Son
68 Old Compton St, W1 (437
2847).
*For almost all foreign and
home newspapers and
magazines.*

For page numbers consult shop index.

ANTIQUES

ANTIQUITIES
Charles Ede

ART DECO AND NOUVEAU
Antiquarius
Butler and Wilson
Chenil Galleries
Chiu
Gallerie 1900
Gilded Lily
Halkin Arcade
John Jesse and Irina Laski
Nigel Milne

ARCHITECTURAL
J. Crotty and Son
Crowther and Son
London Architectural and
Salvage Co
Whiteway and Waldron

AUCTIONS
See Product Section

CARPETS
Bernadout and Bernadout
David Black
Grays Antique Market
C. John
The Rug Shop

CHANDELIERS
Crick

CLOCKS
Antique Hypermarket
E Hollander
H Knowles Brown
Ronald A Lee
Strike One

COINS
Spink

FURNITURE
And So To Bed
Furniture Cave
John Keil
Just Desks
Mallet
Pelham Galleries

GALLERIES
See Product Section

GENERAL
Barrie Quinn
Dragons
Lacquer Chest
Loot
Mollie Evans
Stephen Long

GLASS
WGT Burne
Delmosne
Eric Lineham
Maureen Thompson
Richard Kihl

MARKETS
Alfies
Antiquarius
Antique Hypermarket
Barrett Street Market
Bermondsey Market
Grays Antique Market
Hampstead Antiques
Emporium
Knightsbridge Pavillion
Portobello Market

METALWARE
The Brass Shop
Robert Preston

ORIENTAL
Bluett
Eskenazi
Sparks
Tempus Antiques

POTTERY AND PORCELAIN
Anthony Belton

PRODUCT INDEX

China Choice
Graham and Oxley
Jean Sewell
Mercury Antiques

SCULPTURE
Jeremy Cooper

SILVER
JH Bourdon-Smith
SJ Philips
SJ Shrubsole
Silver Vaults Chancery House

TEXTILES
Grays Antique Market
Gilded Lily
Lunn Antiques
RAU

VICTORIANA
Baylys
Carries

ACQUISITIONS

DOLLS
The Doll Shop
Kaye Desmond

EPHEMERA
Baylys
Carries
Dodo
London Post Card Centre
The Poster Shop
Pleasures of Pastimes
Quadrille
Robert Heron
Vintage Magazine Store
The Workshop

JUKE BOXES
RG Edwards

MUSICAL BOXES
Keith Harding

PENS
Paul Smith
Pencraft
The Penfriend
Philip Poole

RAILWAYS
Collector's Corner

SHELLS
Eaton's Shell Shop
Precious Shells

STAMPS
Harris Publications
Royal Stamp Co
Stanley Gibbons
Stanley Gibbons Auctions

ART & CRAFT SUPPLIES

CAMERAS
Keith Johnson Photographic
Leeds Camera Centre
Techno Cameras

CRAFTS
Bead Warehouse
Candle Makers Supplies
Eatons Shell Shop
Fulham Pottery
Hobby Horse
Yarncraft

GENERAL
Jim Bollom
Buck and Ryan
Chelsea Art Supplies
L Cornelissen
Felt and Hessian Shop
Graphic Art Centre
Paperchase
Reeves
Rowney
Russell and Chapple
Rymans
Times Drawing Office
Wheatsheaf
Windsor and Newton

PRODUCT INDEX

MODELS
Beatties
Patricks
Seagull Model

PAPERS
Falkiners Fine Papers
Paperchase

TAPESTRY AND EMBROIDERY
Danish House
Ehrman
Gloriafilia
Patchwork Dog and Calico Cat
WHI Tapestry Shop

THEATRICAL
Anello and Davide
Brodie and Middleton
Charles H Fox
Davenports
Russell and Chapple
Theatre Zoo

WOOL
Colourspun
Yarncraft
The Yarn Store

BOOKS

ALTERNATIVE
Alternative Bookshop
Atlantis Bookshop
Colletts London Bookshop
Compendium
Corner House Bookshop
Kegan Paul Trench Truber
Other Bookshop
Rudolf Steiner
Theosophical Bookshop
Watkins Bookshop

ANTEQUARIAN
Arthur Page
Bell Book & Radmall
Bertram Rota
Bondy
Francis Edwards
Hatchards
Heywood Hill
Joseph
Maggs
Peter Eaton
Piccadilly Rare Books
Quaritch
Sotherans

ART AND ARCHITECTURE
Arts Council Bookshop
Hatchards
London Art and Academy Bookshop
Photographers Gallery
Sims & Reed
Zwemmer

BOTANICAL
Mary Bland
Joseph
Francis Edwards
Travel Bookshop

CINEMA
The Cinema Bookshop
Vintage Magazine Store

CHILDRENS
Carries
Childrens World
Heywood Hill
Joseph
Lion & Unicorn Bookshop
Paperchase

FANTASY
Forbidden Planet

FASHION
Lesley Hodges

FEMINISM
Compendium
Corner House Bookshop
Sisterwrite

FOREIGN LANGUAGE
Books from India
Collett's Chinese Gallery and Bookshop
Collett's International Bookshop
Foyles
Hachette Librarie Francaise
Orbis
Paperbooks
Zeno

GENERAL — NEW
Angel Bookshop
Belgravia Books
Bernard Stone
Central Books
Compendium
Dillons
Elgin Books
Foyles
Hammicks
Harrods
Hatchards
Heywood Hill
High Hill Bookshop
HMSO
Kensington Bookshop
Kilburn Bookshop
Notting Hill Books
Pan Bookshop
Penguin Bookshop
Truslove and Hanson

GENERAL — SECOND HAND
Arthur Page
Bernard Stone
Central Books
Cobb and Webb Bookshop
Eric and Joan Stevens Booksellers
Heywood Hill
Keith Fawkes and Stanley Smith
Primrose Hill Books
Skoob Books
Studio Bookshop
Vintage Magazine Store

HORSES
J A Allen

NEWSPAPERS
Robert Heron
Moroni and Son

PRIVATE PRESS
Basilisk Press
Bertram Rota

SOCIAL SCIENCE
Dillons
Economist Bookshop
Modern Book Co

THEATRE
Dance Bookshop
Samuel French Theatre Bookshop

TRAVEL
Travel Bookshop
Francis Edwards

CLOTHES

ACCESSORIES
Antiquarius
Badge Shop
Bead Warehouse
Bland and Son
Blax
Brother Sun
Butler and Wilson
Casson
Christopher Trill
Crolla
Detail
Electrum
Fendi
Fenwicks
Glamour City
Harvey Nichols
James Smith
Jarrolds
John Burke
John Jesse and Irina Laski
Joseph

PRODUCT INDEX

Rosslyn Hill Delicatessen

CHOCOLATES
Ackermans Chocolates
Bendicks
Charbonnel & Walker
Clare's Chocolates
Elena
Prestat
Thorntons

COFFEE AND TEA
Algerian Coffee Stores
Drury Tea and Coffee Co
Ferns
H R Higgins
Lodders at the Coffee and Tea Warehouse
Marcus Coffee
Monmouth Coffee House
Richmond Tea and Coffee
Whittards

DELICATESSENS
French
Delices des Gascogne
Hobbes & Co
Justin de Blank
Randall & Aubin
Rilla & Cox
Rosslyn Hill Delicatessen

General
Acquired Taste
Bennetts
Continental Stores
Mr Christians
Old Brompton Colonial
Olga Stores
Partridges
Richmond Hill Delicatessen

German
Bartholdi
German Food Centre
Quality Delicatessen

Italian
G Parmigiani Figli
Hobbs & Co

TRADITIONAL — WOMEN
Burberrys
Ireland House Shop
Jaeger
James Drew
N Peal
Scotch House

UTILITY
Damart
Dance Centre
P Denny
Flak
Flip
Laurence Corner

FOOD

BREAD
Bonne Bouche
Ceres Bakery
Coleson
Di's Larder
Dugdale & Adams
Harrods
Justin de Blank's Hygenic Bakery
Paris Croissant
Patisserie Francaise
Robert Troop
Waitrose

CHEESE
Acquired Taste
Camden Wine & Cheese Centre
Harrods
Justin de Blank
Mainly English
Mr Christians
Paxton & Whitfield

La Ciocciara
Lina Stores
Luigi's
O Bellusci

Greek
Athenian Grocery
Greek Food Centre

Jewish
Rogg
Superfoods
Waitrose

Oriental
Cheon Leen Supermarket
Ganeesha
Golden Orient
Great Wall
Loon Fung Supermarket
Peking Stores
Thai Shop

Scandinavian
Danish Food Centre
Scandinavian Shop
The Swedish Shop

FISH

Bob White
J Mist & Son
Harrods
Leadenhall Market
Richards
Samuel Gordon
Selfridges
Steve Hatt
Wainwright & Daughter

FRUIT AND VEGETABLES
Berwick Street Market
Chapel Street Market
Fortnum & Mason
Hobbs & Co (South Audley St)
Justin de Blank
New Covent Garden
North End Road Market
Shepherds Bush Market
Wainwright & Daughter

GENERAL
Buy Late
Fortnum & Mason
Harrods
Here Is Food
Marks & Spencer
Partridges
Selfridges
The Grocery Shop
24 Hour Supermarket
Waitrose

HEALTH
Chalk Farm Nutrition Centre
Cranks Health Foods
Cranks Whole Grain Shop
Di's Larder
East West Foods
Grocers
Neals Yard
Osaka
Ranbow Groceries

HERBS
Chalk Farm Nutrition Centre
Golden Orient
Greek Food Centre
Justin de Blank's Herbs, Plants
and Flowers Shop
L'Herbier de Provence
Lodders at the Coffee and Tea
Warehouse

MARKETS
Berwick Street Market
Chapel Street Market
Church Street Market
Community Centre Markets
East Street Market
North End Road Market
Portobello Market
Leadenhall Market
New Covent Garden
Shepherds Bush Market
Smithfield
Tachbrook Street Market
The Cut Market

MEAT AND GAME
Bartholdi

181

PRODUCT INDEX

C Lidgate
Druce & Craddock
Harrods
Hundred Acre Farm Shop
John Baily
Leadenhall Market
Leathhams Larder
Randall & Aubin
Slater Cooke Bisney & Jones
W Fenn
Wholefood Butchers

PATISSERIE
Alexis
Bendicks
Bonne Bouche
House of Floris
Kramer
Maison Bertaux
Maison Bouquillon
Marine Ices
Patisserie Francaise
Valerie

WINE
Balls Bros
Bottoms Up
Camden Wine and Cheese
Centre
Great Wapping Wine Co
Mainly English
The Noble Grape
Seven Dials Wine Co

HOME

ANIMALS
Animal Fair
Brick Lane
Harrods
Palmers

ARCHITECTURAL
Acquisitions
London Architectural Salvage
and Supply Co
Whiteway & Waldron

BASKETS
David Mellor
Forces Help Society and Lord
Roberts Workshops
Graham & Green
Inca
Yvonne Peters

BATHROOM
Crabtree & Evelyn
Floris
L'Herbier de Provence
London Architectural Salvage
and Supply Co
Penhaligons
Sitting Pretty
Virginia
Yves Rocher

BEDROOM
After Dark
And So To Bed
Bedlam
Dennis Groves
Domat Designs
Futon Company
Heals
Kermessee
London Bedding Centre
One Off
The Bedchamber
The Space Saving Bed Centre
Upstairs Shop

BLINDS
Blind Alley
Cargo
Habitat
John Lewis

CANDLES
The Candles Shop
John Lewis

CARPETS AND RUGS
Afia Carpets
Astrohome
Cargo
Casa Pupo
Habitat

Resista Carpets

CHINA
Divertimenti
Casa Pupo
Casa Fina
General Trading Co
Graham & Green
Habitat
Nina Campbell
Reject China Shop
Reject Shop
Reject Shop Hardware
Richard Dare
Strangeways

COOKERS AND STOVES
Buyers and Sellers
Cooker Centre
John Lewis
The London Stove Centre
The Stove Centre

CHEMISTS
Bliss
Boots
John Bell & Croydon
Warman & Freed

CRAFTS
Byzantium
Campion
Covent Garden Market
Craftsmen Potters Association
David Mellor
East Asia Co
Inca
Liberty's
Lock Shop
Naturally British
Neal Street Shop
The Glasshouse

ELECTRICAL
Barkers
Houndsditch
John Lewis

FURNITURE
Antique
See Product Section

Painted
Dragons
Hippo Hall
Shop For Painted Furniture

Office
Hubbards
Practical Styling
Rymans

Modern
Adeptus
Aram Designs
Astrohome
Co Existence
Conran
Dennis Groves
General Trading Co
Habitat
Heals
Homeworks
Just Sofas
Libertys
One Off
Practical Styling

Pine
Geranium
Habitat
Kermessee
Merchant Chandler
Pine Mine
Sophistocat
The Pine Shop

Second Hand
See also Auction and
Antiques
Furniture Cave
Portobello Market
Rau
Salvation Army
Second Hand City

GAMES
The Chess Centre

183

PRODUCT INDEX

RECORDS
Beggar's Banquet
Collector's Corner
Dobbells
Harold Moore Records
HMV
James Asman
Rough Trade
That's Entertainment
Vintage Record Centre
Virgin Records

SERVICES
See Services Section

SECOND HAND/JUNK
See also Markets, Auctions
Alfie's Antique Market
Brick Lane Market
Camden Lock
Davy
Gilded Lily
Lost Property Sales
Naylor's
Oddity's
Old Kent Road
Portobello Market
Salvation Army
Second Hand City
Twentieth Century Box

STATIONERY
Brats
Chisolms
Dilemma
Nina Campbell
Paperchase
Pen to Paper Shop
Scribblers
Smythson
Strangeways
Walton Street Stationery Co

TELEPHONES
The Telephone Shop

TILES
Cane and Table
Casa Catalan
Sitting Pretty

Tile Reject Shop
Townsends

TOBACCO
Astleys
Fribourg and Treyer
Smokes
Sullivan Powell

TOOLS
Buck and Ryan

TOYS
Carries
Children's World
Davenport's
Domat Designs
Doll's House
Dragons
Eric Snook
Galt Toys
Hamleys
Heals
Kite Store
Knutz
Kristin Baybars
Patrick's
Pierrot
Pollocks Toy Museum
The Singing Tree
Tiger Moth
Tiger Tiger

WALLPAPER & FABRIC
Colefax and Fowler Chintz
Shop
Coles
Designer's Guild
Felt and Hessian Shop
John Lewis
John Oliver
Just Gingham
Laura Ashley
Liberty's
Liberty's Print Shop
Mary Fox Linton
Moorehouse Associates
Nice Irma's Floating Carpet
Osborne and Little
Patchwork Dog and Calico Ca

PRODUCT INDEX

Peacock
Rain
Upstairs Shop

WOOL
Colourspun
Danish House
The Yarn Store
WHI Tapestry

SPORTS

BICYCLES
Alans Cycles
E J Barnes
Bell St Bikes
Beta Bikes
Condor Cycles
Covent Garden Cycles
General Auctions
Tandem
The Victoria Cycling Co

BOATS
Boat Showrooms of London
Inflatable Boat Centre
London Dinghy Centre
Proctor
Tony Williams

CAMPING
Blacks
YHA Shop

DANCE
Anello and Davide
Dance Centre
Gamba
Pineapple Dance Centre

FISHING
Farlowes
House of Hardy

GENERAL
Alpine Sports
Hamleys
Harrods
Lillywhites

Pindisports

GUNS
Bland and Son

RIDING
George Parkes
The Huntsman
Moss Bros

SPECIALIST
Archery Centre
Captain O M Watts
The Chess Centre
Games Centre
Giddens
Kite Store
Kite and Balloon Co
Just Games
Lewis Leathers
Queen's Ice Rink Shop
The Racket Shop
Slick Willies
Sports Drobny
Swaine, Adeney and Briggs
Thames Water Sports
Thurston and Co
Village Games

SHOES
Cobra

SKIING
Alpine Sports
Harrods
Lilleywhites
Pindisports
Sun And Snow

187

SHOP INDEX

SHOP INDEX

SHOP INDEX

SHOP INDEX

SHOP INDEX

194

SHOP INDEX

TRANSPORT

Public transport operates to many parts of London throughout the night, so before you decide to spend pounds on a cab or risk using the car, find out what is available.

The last Underground trains leave the West End after midnight with some such as the Piccadilly Line from Piccadilly Circus as late as 12.30am. Most of the last journeys on the main bus routes leave central London in the half hour before midnight.

However some of the well know routes (such as the 11) run all night and their is also a network of special night bus services which operate throughout the night which should get you at least part of the way home. To check for details for routes and times phone London Transport's 24 hour Travel Information service on 01 222 1234.

There are still a few early morning trains on some lines in the British Rail network. Telephone your local enquiry bureau for details.

London Transport produce a useful comprehensive booklet with details of all the all-night buses and other public transport facilities which operate in the small hours. You should be able to get a copy from any of London Transport's Travel Information Centres or by post from the Public Relations Officer, 55 Broadway, London SW1H 0BD.

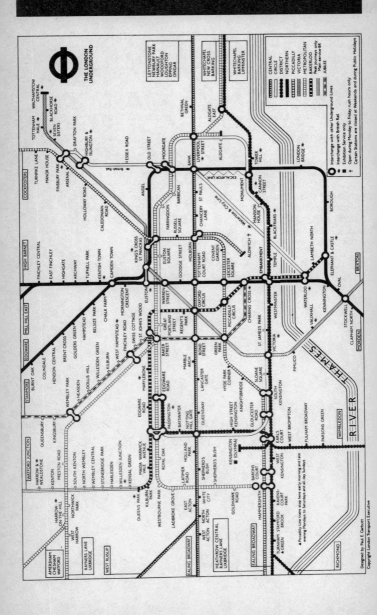

THE LONDON UNDERGROUND

Designed by Paul E. Garbutt
Copyright London Transport Executive